The
CHANGING WEST

An Economic Theory About Our Golden Age

By
WILLIAM ALLEN WHITE

☆

NEW YORK
THE MACMILLAN COMPANY
1939

Copyright, 1939, by
THE MACMILLAN COMPANY.

All rights reserved—no part of this book may be reproduced in any form without permission in writing from the publisher, except by a reviewer who wishes to quote brief passages in connection with a review written for inclusion in magazine or newspaper.

*Set up and electrotyped. Published **November, 1939**.*
*Reprinted November, 1939 **(twice)**.*

PRINTED IN THE UNITED STATES OF AMERICA
AMERICAN BOOK—STRATFORD PRESS, INC., NEW YORK

PREFACE

THIS book had its inception in a series of lectures delivered at Harvard University before the Extracurricular Committee in the Department of American History. The committee, inviting me to speak, suggested that I talk about the changing West. Chewing the matter over for a month or two, it occurred to me that Americans might have to revise their theories about the old West and its mainsprings and impulses. We have been told by one group of historians that in so far as the West was unique its peculiarities arose from the fact that into the West only the brave and adventurous came for 150 years as the pioneers moved swiftly across the continent beyond the thirteen colonies. Their courage and enterprise, according to the heroic theory, gave the West its character. Another group of historians emphasize the fact that the vicissitudes of our western border life developed latent qualities in men and women—qualities of hardihood, of imagination, of capacity, initiative, industry, of thrift, prudence, and so on—that made a race of supermen on the prairies and the plains, in the mountains and on the golden slopes of the Pacific.

Certainly the constantly moving frontier, which was a hundred years going from Pittsburgh to Los Angeles, did make a civilization of its own kind, a golden age here in the American West. I do not know from what ore and soil and circumstances the West was mined and smelted, but I feel that our golden age was not built by supermen sifted out of the East and from Europe. I feel that neither did the hardships of the frontier weld men from dross to steel. It shall be the thesis of this book that the West became what it was because of a vast increment of wealth from the rising price of the virgin land of the twenty-four states that were erected beyond our western colonial border in the nineteenth century. This tremendous increment, transmuted by the democratic process into fluid capital according to the thesis upon which this book is written, was distributed economically and digested socially, also by the democratic processes, by literate people who were as nearly absolutely free as it was possible in the nineteenth century for any man to be free. Alas, I have no statistics with which to back up this thesis. I am a country editor not a trained economist. Economists may come along and shatter the hypothesis. But here it is, the story of America's golden age as I have seen it through at least seven decades of the fifteen in which the West was unfolding: the vast magic carpet of prairie and plain and mountain, of lakes and rivers, deserts and forests, all yielding their wealth which was bent more or less consciously to the purposes of free and aspiring men. It was a new thing in God's world, a strange and beautiful thing, this unfolding of the golden West. Other lands, in other migratory periods of history, have yielded great wealth.

PREFACE

But the settlement of the western United States offers a first and shining example of a free people, morally and intellectually literate, using their own devices, their own sense of justice, to develop the wealth of a region and to distribute it as a common wealth. I may be wrong about the spiritual secret of the mainsprings of this unfolding of wealth controlled and directed by the democratic ideal of justice; but as a reporter I have tried to tell a straight story about the outward and visible way the mainspring worked which moved men westward in a widening, deepening stream of social and economic justice. I must make acknowledgments to the *Yale Review* and to the *Survey Graphic* for permitting the use of Chapters III and IV, which were taken from these magazines and recast somewhat for this volume.

W. A. White

Emporia, Kansas
October 15, 1939

CONTENTS

		PAGE
Preface		v

CHAPTER

I.	The West That Was	1
II.	The West That Is	25
III.	The Peculiar Problem of the West	59
IV.	How Far Have We Come—and Why?	80
V.	How May the West Survive?	107
VI.	The Net of It	139

THE CHANGING WEST

I

THE WEST THAT WAS

THE first point that should be made clear in a discussion of the West is a definition of the West. An accurate definition of the West should be in terms of geography and time. Geographically the term "West" used in these pages will mean the territory west of Buffalo and Pittsburgh, north of the Ohio River, onward to the Pacific Coast from Los Angeles to Seattle. In time, let us assume that the settlement of the West began about the time of the adoption of the Constitution of the United States and that the West gradually has been settled in the area described above during the century and a half that ended in the first third of the twentieth century.

Here are twenty-four states regionally divided something like this: the basin of the Great Lakes comprising five states, Ohio, Indiana, Illinois, Michigan, and Wisconsin; the trans-Mississippi country, Minnesota, Iowa, Missouri, Oklahoma—more or less—Kansas, Nebraska, and the Dakotas; the Rocky Mountain states, Montana, Wyoming, Colorado, New Mexico, Arizona, Utah, Nevada, Idaho; and the Pacific Coast states, Washington, Oregon, and California. That is the continental West, geographically limited by the boundaries of the American Republic. The South was, a century and a half ago, and is now, another region. It was another area because its civilization was builded upon an idea rather different from the sectional philosophy of the West, and so in the South another civilization developed, somewhat different from the civilization of the West.

I shall try to present the story of the growth of the West, not entirely as a geographical region, but as an economic evolutionary process, if you will. I shall try to define the West, considered as a cultural ground where the growth of human liberty under the economic conditions peculiar to our pioneer development has given direction and marked its path to a sectional civilization.

Something like one hundred and twenty-five years ago, my grandfather, John White, born in Massachusetts, came out of northern New York in a mover's wagon with his family of six or eight children and headed for the Western Reserve in Ohio. John White so exactly typifies the early western pioneer that I must pause here to tell you something about him. This grandfather of mine, John White, was the son of another John White, my great-grandfather, a Revolutionary soldier. My grandfather was born during the Revolutionary War. The White family had lived in Massachusetts around Taunton, in Raynham, since the middle 1630's. They had been town clerks and officers in the Congregational Church, farmers, mechanics, storekeepers with an occasional preacher in the lot,

THE WEST THAT WAS

and were all good middle-class Puritans. The Whites moved in the mill run of Yankee civilization. When my grandfather, John White, was in his early manhood—along about 1797, to be exact—he married Fear Perry, who lived at Lee, Massachusetts; and within a few years, John White and Fear Perry struck out from Lee and established themselves in what was then a wild country in northern New York. John set up a little forge—part blacksmith shop, part iron foundry. Either because the country was getting too thickly settled, or because he had an itching foot, John and Fear left this new country in New York for the wilder country of northern Ohio. They settled at Norwalk, Ohio, about fifty miles southwest of Cleveland. They settled on land for which they paid a dollar an acre! They spent two decades clearing the land of timber and draining it. When John and Fear died the land was worth thirteen dollars an acre, for it was a good piece of bottom land. Their children came thick and fast until there were thirteen of them. John and Fear were prosperous, diligent, thrifty Yankees. In northern Ohio they were able to give their thirteen children the best education that the pioneer environment afforded, and their sons and daughters, most of them, settled in Huron County, or near-by places, and became merchants, lawyers, doctors, and traders.

So much for what they were. Now as to their kit and accouterment. When their caravan in northern New York started to move—a covered wagon, a few children, a little livestock—they had in that outfit practically nothing that Abraham did not have when he and his tribe trekked out of the land of Ur three thousand years before. John and Fear had the tamed horse, the tamed cow, the domestic chicken, and the tamed pig. They had fire and the lever and the wheel. The wheel was a little further developed than the wheel as Abraham knew it, but still it was the wheel. They had textiles. Fear Perry wove the wool that made the garments of her family. She knew the secrets of dyeing that the mothers in Israel knew. And John could work with iron and hammer at steel. Perhaps John's plow was better than the plows that Abraham saw in the valley farms of his day. But the difference between that outfit which John White and Fear Perry carried with them from northern New York to the lake region, and the earlier implements of the hearth and the herd which Abraham and Sarah used, was striking only in two things: John and Fear had gunpowder and the printed word. Except for the gun and the book, Abraham with a little tinkering would have been able to understand everything that John had in his covered wagon. But spiritually, the difference between the attitudes of mind and heart of John and his tribe and Abraham and his tribe represented the progress of three thousand years. It was the spiritual environment of men in those two great treks—the one led by Abraham out of the land of Ur and the other of which John White was a part, coming from New England and the Atlantic coastal states into the new lands of the West—that defines the essential differences between the two civilizations which grew up in the Val-

THE WEST THAT WAS

ley of the Euphrates and in the Valley of the Mississippi. John and Fear had attained in a large measure something which Abraham and Sarah felt only as a vague yearning. It was the thing called liberty and the definite love of it.

If Abraham had moved into the Mississippi Valley under the political environment and spiritual limitations of his own time, he would have created in our West something like the kind of civilization that Abraham's seed set up later in the land of Canaan. As a matter of fact, the attitude toward the aborigines of John and Fear and the attitude of the thousands that were crossing the Alleghenies and the Appalachians in the West one hundred and fifty years ago was about the same attitude that Abraham's seed held toward the Canaanites. Both sets of pioneers wiped out the occupants of the land and set up their own social order. But it is the social order which the children of New England established after driving away and wiping out the original owners of the land that marks the difference between Abraham's pastoral civilization and an agrarian rural civilization which later merged into the American industrial empire. It is that West which during a century and a half John and Fear erected along with their heirs and assigns that concerns us today.

Why, we may ask, was that West which they made here in these wide valleys, across these bleak deserts, beyond these gorgeous rugged Rockies and on down into the soft and lovely lands along the western ocean, so different a civilization from that which the ancient pioneers established in the valleys of the Nile, the Euphrates, and the Ganges? You will reply, of course, quickly, that machines made the difference. But what checked the establishment of machines in the valleys of the Nile, the Euphrates, and the Ganges? Machines were set up before the nineteenth century—primitive machines which for a thousand years and more remained primitive while other pioneers moved into other lands. Why did these simple, mechanical devices that John and Fear knew begin suddenly to multiply in their pioneering days of the nineteenth century? Why did these machines not only begin to multiply but begin to beget new machines more powerful, more complex, which in turn brought forth new machines in iron and steel, stone and copper, and still newer and stranger devices of a stuff not made with hands? I mean legal machines, social machines, economic machines all whirring in unison—the steel levers, the wheels, and the cogs clicking in the meshes made by the new political, financial, social gadgets and inventions that set up a new way of life. The new way of life spread into the valleys of the Ohio, the Mississippi, the Missouri, the Snake, the Columbia, the Sacramento, and down the little dry streams that in the rainy season go rushing through the sands of southern California to the sea. Why have the machines, material and intangible, established themselves as the very basis of this western civilization of ours? And in passing, we may ask why these machines, physical and spiritual, have been un-

THE WEST THAT WAS

able to penetrate so completely into the civilization of other lands which physically are not unlike our land.

Let me try to answer. It seems to me that John and Fear had something in their covered wagon that was a new thing in the pioneering world. For the first time pioneers had stood upon the mountaintops overlooking rich, noble lands and had brought with them to enlarge their vision a philosophy which was to establish a way of life that never before had risen above the plow of other pioneers.

"Pioneers O Pioneers!"

It was a great trek, that flood of immigrants that swept into the Mississippi Valley, across the Rockies, and down the western slopes of the continent in the hundred and fifty years that followed the adoption of the American Constitution. It was comparable to the waves of population that must have come out of Asia into western Europe two thousand years ago. It was comparable to the flight of the Spaniards in the sixteenth and seventeenth centuries to South America. But these pioneers of the West in the United States differed from most other pioneers in this: They were free men, these American westerners, free bodies, free spirits. No king could tax them. They did not have to bear arms for any tyrant. They could worship God as they pleased. They could establish their own form of government without let or hindrance. They had the right of trial by jury and carried with them the writ of habeas corpus. They had their personal freedoms, of speech, of conscience, of the press, and the right of assembly. As for economic freedom, it began at the bottom; each pioneer family fared well or ill somewhat according to its own application of courage, intelligence, and industry. The western pioneers of the eighteenth and nineteenth centuries had even more legal rights than their forebears had who crossed the seas in the seventeenth and eighteenth centuries. For the Pilgrims and the Puritans and their neighbors in New York and the other North American colonies, fought for their freedom after they got here. These western pioneers of the eighteenth and nineteenth centuries, the children of the Colonists, fought only with the forces of the wilderness and fought not for freedom—they had that—but for security. The civilization which the pioneers of the nineteenth century set up out beyond the Alleghenies on across the land was unique.

It is true, of course, that the pioneers of our nineteenth century West were no freer in their West than their fathers whom they left behind in the New England and Atlantic coastal states. But the western pioneers had this much that the home folks in New England and the middle states and the south did not have —a new, rich land, a raw, free country. The pioneers of the nineteenth century West were unimpeded by economic inequalities save those that were inherent in the qualities of men. There in this West of ours, for the first time on earth, a free people worked at their own political and social salvation. Now it is vital to

THE WEST THAT WAS

understand two spiritual circumstances that made the population of the West unique: The westerner, first of all, was free to think and speak as he pleased; and, secondly, he was of the kind that demanded that what he earned should be his very own.

Growing out of these freedoms, spiritual and economic, were two other typical, indeed two deeply symbolical institutions that appeared in every village and township as the tides of population moved toward the setting sun: The schoolhouse and the church were the first institutional establishments to be housed by any pioneer community. The church stripped of its gaudy theological trappings—and they were gaudy indeed—starkly stood for the morals of the community. The morals of the community grew out of a yearning for justice, the striving of men toward an ideal of human relations. Of course the striving was toward a sadly unrealized ideal. But the aspiration in the hearts of the pioneers, as they organized and established the work of their hands and their houses of worship, represented as concretely as anything could embody it their relation to the forces outside themselves which they felt made for righteousness and which they called God. Their God was a spirit—an ideal—as unreal and as unapproachable as justice, peace, love, liberty, mercy, judgment, or wisdom. Yet he was quite as real in their lives as these other aspirations. In their tabernacles, little white box-shaped structures with spires at one end, they set up their gods who impersonated their pioneer ethical ideals, and out of those ideals of human conduct they built their land, they wrote their laws, they achieved under their tribal God such of these ideals as they could tolerably comprehend.

The church represented the thirst for righteousness which, in the lingo of their theology, they called the Kingdom of God. I know how far they failed to live up to their ideals, of course. There were thieves and adulterers and murderers, covetous persons and hypocrites and liars among the pioneers; just as many as they left at home by the cold hearths of their deserted firesides. And in the free country of the West opportunities for scoundrels were wider than at home. The talent that made a common cheat in a New England town, created a robber baron out West. If men took the religion of their homes into the wilderness, they also took their vices. But the point is, they did take a religion which contained an ethic and plan for human relations based essentially on a hazy vision of liberty. Liberty is one thing you can't have unless you give it to others. A man does not establish free institutions unless he has faith in his fellow men. The religion of the pioneers was founded upon the profound faith in others that implied the acceptance of the Golden Rule, the greatest of the Commandments. Being a human society, it was imperfect. The ideals of the western pioneers slipped a lot. But the social contract based upon so-called Christian ideals did establish freedom without thought of allegiance to kings or to churchly orders and did set up freedom in a land where the individual's own talents gave him his place among his fellows. That religion of the pioneer was

THE WEST THAT WAS

the spiritual structure upon which the laws of the West were based, and from which the institutions of the West grew. Every man believed doctrinally what he pleased. But under the theory of liberty which the Western pioneers cherished, every man earned what he got, and approximately got what he earned. Moreover, the economic atmosphere in which the American pioneer moved was heavy with potential riches —his own riches if he could get them! That was a new thing in the pioneering world.

Then the pioneers of the first frontiers of our country set up another institution to check the church. For these pioneers of the new West would have no theocracy. So the little red schoolhouse appeared wherever a dozen families stopped to build a neighborhood. The school represented the pioneer's contact with reality. Here was the pioneer's temple of research. Here was the challenge to moral, political, and economic stagnation. The schoolhouse, teaching its simple rules of reading and writing and arithmetic became the basis of material progress. Out of the schoolhouse rose the college and its laboratory and the private and public bureaus of research. In the schoolhouse dire necessity to move upward from a simple to a more complex civilization found encouragement. The mother of invention was well nourished there in the little red schoolhouse by the road. Her milk suckled a race of giants who often threatened to capture the country. For some of them were inordinately acquisitive. But the western people sometimes were too strong for their giants. In any case out of those two tiny, rude, primitive edifices, the little white church and the little red schoolhouse, rose liberty of action, which was the architect of the spiritual structures of our western civilization.

If we understand the West it will pay us to examine the stuff which came forth from these two temples. For instance: What was this Christian religion which had its various tabernacles of many denominations that the pioneers built in the western wilderness? Well, first of all, it was a religion of optimism. The ethics of Jesus of Nazareth are essentially hopeful because they require faith in man. He taught men that the good neighbor will be happy but not entirely in the possession of worldly goods. Certainly his happiness will not come at all because physical laws will bend themselves to the good neighbor's prayers. The physical world is outside the religion of Jesus. The religion of Jesus is in its essence entirely a religion of the spirit. This was the great truth which Jesus revealed to the woman of Samaria at the well, and which he chose to reveal to that rather simple person, not to a priest nor to a wise man. Alas, the religious creed in these little churches of many fields—the Methodists, the Campbellites, the Presbyterians, the Baptists, the Congregationalists, the Episcopalians—which the pioneers set up as they fought their way across the land, was channeled superficially on the one hand by the fear of hell and on the other hand by the hope of reward in heaven. But that surface channeling did not change the fact that the religion of the new West was essentially and in its deeper currents a religion of optimism and a profound faith that kindness pays in the deeper satisfactions of the human heart. It is tremendously important, in understanding the West, to know this: that the western people built upon this optimism. They built upon this ideal for the first time unrestrained by the religious faith of kings, by the power or influence of any formal religion of authority. With free consciences they established their own authority. They built their own life. And they were checked and directed in the purposes of their faith and freedom only by the practical common sense that came from formal education which they established co-ordinately with the church. The school and the church were supported entirely in their own neighborhoods. Each institution grew apart from the other. This separation kept the spiritual ideals of a people from cramping the growth of the institutions which exclusively concerned and developed the physical world. Those were the two basic free institutions—the church and the school—upon which the West was built, a unique civilization in the earth, a new thing for mankind.

It is hard to tell which was the cart and which the horse in this team of freedom: in one yoke, a folk church, and a folk school in another yoke. Perhaps a free church and a free school developed the political freedom which characterized the settlement in the West. Perhaps the freedom which the settlers knew when they crossed the mountains into the great valley and swept over the hills toward the western sea, urged them to establish and maintain separately the free church and the free school. But upon these freedoms —whichever came first—I shall try to prove the West built its economic foundation. Upon this foundation the West erected its unique social order.

I seriously doubt if the thesis can be maintained that the American West drew from our Atlantic seaboard men and women who were especially adventurous. The West drew all kinds of people; the adventurous, of course, but not all of them. The shiftless and lazy came West who could not quite make it go in the established order of New England and the middle Atlantic states. Also the ordinary citizen who wished to better his condition joined the western caravan, and all these, the good, the bad, the indifferent, joined the long procession that wound its way westward at the turn of the eighteenth century—the caravan which kept moving for nearly a hundred years. Again I feel sure it was not the hardships and deprivations of pioneer life that gave the West its character. Though of course deprivations were goads which kept a free people moving forward. We shall have to look further than the alleged select character of the western population and elsewhere than in the privations and hardships of the times and circumstances of pioneer life, to account for the unique spiritual qualities—good and bad—and to account for the peculiar material aspects of our midcontinental civilization. Nor were the differences between the West on the one hand and the East and South on the other due to the fact that the westward-moving procession was joined by Scandinavians and Germans in the latter half of the nineteenth century.

The outward and visible sectional differences in the United States were twofold: First, the new settlers of the West, enjoying their new spiritual freedom and erecting political institutions to safeguard their freedom, found wider opportunity for material success in the West than in their former homes. Good jobs in the West were comparatively easy to get. An indifferent man could go further with his five talents in the West where the man-market was not overcrowded, than he could go in the East. The talented man found free play for his executive imagination. The ne'er-do-well sometimes woke up as luck touched him with its golden wand. As a miner, the shiftless man might strike it rich. As a landowner, he could find a fertile quarter-section. As a trader, the odds were always in his favor in a country where an expanding economy during the nineteenth century made an ascending spiral of prosperity. But over all, above all, and through all was the second factor of western change and growth —the gorgeous economic fact that cheap land, when it was occupied by the pioneers, was constantly becoming more and more valuable. The increment of land values bestowed by the billions on a free people was directed by them without tithe or tax or tribute of any kind to an absentee king or potentate. This incremental wealth of an awakening continent was controlled entirely by the social, the commercial, and the political institutions of an independent people. These pioneers, giving impulse and purpose to this vast heritage of new capital, established a new civilization—somewhat a new kind of civilization in the new West. For the first time on earth in a new country liberty and literacy, the little white church beside the little red schoolhouse set up their own dominion. It was in theory democratic—this definite yearning for liberty and a kind of equality. The pioneers built upon the fabulous imperial wealth at once created and largely distributed under those free forces. In detail that statement means this: that the material wealth of the West, the wealth that came from the land and the rise in the price of land, the farms, the forests, the mines, created a base of fluid capital. That capital structure operated by a free people, literate morally and politically civilized, became the basis for an enormous expansion of credit—a safe basis for this huge volume of quasi currency. With that expanded credit based upon the faith of man in man, the heritage of the little white church, investments were possible which produced labor-saving machines, increased man's output and further enlarged man's wealth and still further made credit expansion wise and stable. Of course, periods of economic folly came. Of course, the rising spiral of prosperity had many cyclical periods of depression. But also the eternal wellspring of rising land values controlled by the civilized influences of a free economy did, for a century and a half, create a fund which made liberty possible, which set up a democratic fraternity which in turn established some kind of economic equality and made justice approximately possible. All these set American freedom up in business as a going concern that paid. That going concern made the West.

Finding the "Pearl of Great Price"

The princely increment of land values constantly rising for a century and a half, multiplied by the unrestricted enterprise of a free people, established an impregnable fortress of capital not only for the West but for all America. That capital was distributed by democracy—the philosophy of the little white church, joined to the universal literacy and that incidental intelligence which came out of the little red schoolhouse. Capital, stored up but distributed in ownership with an approximation of fairness, capital from this continental treasure house, this capital even clumsily and often wickedly directed by the rough ethics of democracy, built up the golden West of our golden era. It was a new economy!

Now how was this capital distributed, arising somewhat from the increment of the land? It was kept fluid by a system of credit which in the nineteenth century became the lubrication of the machine age. Credit is faith—faith that men will keep their promises. Credit is the applied optimism which distinguishes the philosophy of Jesus from "the eternal nay," the fundamental negation of human goodness at the base of other great religious philosophies. World credit waited upon the coming of Christendom. In our American

West, the faith of the pioneers took the huge increment of the land which in other days and times had become the hoardings of the few and built it into the democratic credit structure of a modern world. So the billions of wealth that followed the settlement of the West became capital investment—largely private property, somewhat public. The machine age with all its blessing and also with all its inevitable inequities, was the fruit of that imperfect human nature which in turn was and is the flower of so-called Christian civilization. The essential optimism of democracy stems out of a faith in man's general decency which gave Jesus courage in his last conscious hour at Golgotha: "Father, forgive them; for they know not what they do!" The quest for Utopian justice failed in the West, of course. It always will fail until individual men, living in some dull millennial perfection, develop a sense of duty that will stand the stress and strain of Utopian freedom. But the West, distributing in fluid capital its fabulous gains, after all did set up a structure of credit under the spiritual guidance of the little white church, with material push and drive that was generated in the little red schoolhouse. So the West went about as far toward the Golden Age as men could go with the human limitations of their blood and environment.

Hence we had the gorgeous lure of the West. For the rise in the price of land, the fabulous fortunes from the mines and from virgin forest and from prairie and bleak high plains, added billions upon billions to the wealth of the West, and inevitably gave a majority

THE WEST THAT WAS

of the western people economic security more amply than might have been theirs if they had remained at home near the Atlantic coast. This power of wealth seemed to inflate western personality. In the midst of the nineteenth century, the same talent in a New England village and in Chicago, for instance, yielded different rewards. Something resembling real economic freedom prevailed in the growing West during the nineteenth century. Based upon the rising prices of land—land in farms, in mines, in forests—great fortunes were made by ordinary men, most ordinary men. It was a paradise of swindlers. Feudal overlords arose at the head of every commodity industry—transportation, communication, fuel, timber, oil, the hard metals, banking, milling, and every commercial process which turned raw materials into finished products. For, alas, the freedom men had and the power of wealth did not affect seriously the morals of those who were instinctively grabbers and gougers. These things, freedom and power, merely ballooned the ego of westerners. They could not see the crudity and the vulgarity of much that they were doing. Their sense of duty had not grown up to their sense of importance.

But free men found their hands untied and found their lives unhampered by prejudice, by debt, or by unjust taxes. Free men could accept for the widest use the new labor-saving machines which in the first half of the nineteenth century were beginning to change the world. Not in Europe in those years did the machine age work its greatest miracles, nor in the South, nor even in the industrial East, which set up looms, of course, and furnaces. But out West change straddled the steam engine and galloped to glory.

Two inventions hastened the growth of civilization, and in the western United States speeded up progress more than elsewhere. The two inventions were the steam engine and the unlimited corporation. The one was useful in getting power out of fuel. The other multiplied the power of man's brain. They were uniquely useful in the West, first because of this latent capital arising from the increment of land values, but in the second place and chiefly because the spiritual soil of the West was ready for the universal organization of capital.

The corporation is another of those devices of man —like credit—which at bottom is cemented by faith. Faith in what? Faith in man; faith that men will keep their word. This will bear repeating. This faith implements capital as a servant of human welfare and permeates the fabric of democracy. The spirit of liberty which cherishes the rights of others to save their own is the same spirit that sustains credit and gives power and force to the corporation. Political democracy, capitalism and the so-called Christian ethics are all off one piece of goods. Together they become one manifestation of the power of man's institutionalized faith. Only where men have learned to work together in the practical belief that man on the whole is honest and is kind, will democracy and capitalism thrive. Without faith in that vision, the people perish. It was somewhat because the West was free, it was because the West had the faith of the little white church (crude and sometimes barbarous as some of its external trappings were), and had the wisdom of the little red schoolhouse, primitive as it was, that the machine age came so quickly and so marvelously into the wilderness of the North American continent. Democratic intelligence almost unconsciously harnessed the western increment of the land and made it fluid capital which in turn remade the western United States in a century and a half.

Into the West, of course, with these three forces of modern civilization: (a) the practical acceptance of the Christian philosophy and its corollary tenets of (b) credit and (c) democracy, corruption came because man is human. Politics were sometimes dirty, but only as dirty as men were lazy, dumb, and greedy. Corporations were often venal. Priests and professors of religion were too often hypocrites, and formal religion at times shamed its God and mocked its faith. But the net of it, which gave the West its glory, was good—as good as man!

The moral progress made by the West was reflected in the rise of institutions which protected the weak: manhood suffrage, the abolition of slavery, the right to hold the homestead against debt, free state universities for the common people, commissions and courts for the redress of economic wrongs, such as rebates and trade discriminations of various sorts. The West thus kept its rising wealth in land increment decently but of course not perfectly broken up. The hacienda system which cursed Latin America found no foothold in the United States. Then also, in the West, in the last quarter of the old century and in the first quarter of the new, democratic institutions appeared, like honest ballot laws, primary elections, the direct election of United States Senators, the initiative and referendum; democratic weapons by which the people ardently hoped that economic justice might be secured. It may have been an illusion, but there seemed to be in the West of the last quarter of the nineteenth century a sense of political freedom, along with the economic freedom which marked some distinction at least between the sections. Of course with the opening of this princely treasure house with its billions prodigally scattered among the pioneers, man could afford freedom. Freedom and poverty rarely marry and are easily divorced.

Gradually the free western-born institutions went East and were considered and sometimes adopted and generally improved in the older states. But free institutions moved more easily and rose more swiftly—which may not be a virtue—in the West than in the East.

Which brings us to another distinction of the old West: it was a rural civilization; and, barring certain spots where industry is congested, the West still is a rural civilization today. In less than half a dozen states of the West do the urban centers control the legislatures and dominate state politics. The rural countryside and the country town have the controlling majority in these states. Rural problems—to be exact, the

THE WEST THAT WAS

so-called farm problem in its many forms *—dominate the politics of the West.

By the 1890's, the West was open. The homesteads were all taken out of the public domain. The pioneer days of the land seeker were practically closed. The states of the western empire were for the most part hewed out, the cities established, the transcontinental railroads finished, and the streams of pipes and wires whereupon a great commerce was flowing were completed in the West. The steady, dependable rise in the price of land was finished by the turn of the century. Speculative land booms after that brought collapse and disaster. The unearned increment in the price of land could no longer be depended upon as a secure source of universal prosperity.

The day that closed the homesteading, grub-staking, timber-claiming era, also marked the entrance of national leaders who realized that the economic problems and the political questions arising from promoting the wider production of goods were now no longer paramount. Men like Bryan, Altgeld, La Follette, the first Roosevelt and a score of agrarian leaders like George

* Of which more, later. As a footnote to this statement, it is interesting to observe that in the decade of the 1930's American liberal leaders have come from east of the Alleghenies. This is true largely because the crucial problems of the second quarter of our century are industrial problems, urban problems, problems arising out of the need to give to labor a broader status as a consumer rather than to treat labor as a commodity. But this is beside the point. It is mentioned in passing only to emphasize the differences in the two regions divided roughly by the Alleghenies and the Ohio River.

Norris, William E. Borah, Jonathan Dolliver, Hiram Johnson, arose and found their followers in the West during the two decades at the century's turn. These liberal leaders marked a new era in American political affairs. They were the prophets of discontent who flouted the established order. They and their kind gave political color to the West in the twentieth century. They came only because in the West the vast income that had risen for a hundred years from unearned increment of land was gone, gone apparently forever. These liberal western leaders had their day and time, when they walked in a little brief authority representing the West that was. They were indignant leaders of a baffled people who did not understand that the day of the pioneer with his freedom and with all the blessings which bought his freedom—that day was done. The West as a speculative real estate subdivision on the American map was finished. A new day was at hand, a new problem in politics arising from a realization of a new problem in economics appeared in the United States with the beginning of the fourth decade of the new century. So today, let us leave the West that was, and look for a chapter or so at the West that is. It remains a region. Still it is a state of mind. It is a gay, nostalgic hallucination hanging over from a vast economic stimulation when men believed that they could establish free institutions and pay for them out of profits. Still the West is a spiritual principality, in this nation. The West, even at the threshold of the twentieth century's fifth decade, is of its own kind, having its unique place in a new, strange world.

II

THE WEST THAT IS

AFTER considering our American West geographically and historically it is well to consider it as it is today. Let us ask and answer. What is the West as we know it in the midst of the twentieth century? Its geographical metes and bounds may be easily established. The West is the country north of Mason and Dixon's line, settled in the last century and a half not by the American colonists but by the pioneers. It lies between Buffalo and Los Angeles and between Portland, Oregon, and Pittsburgh, twenty-four states added to the original thirteen. Each state differs slightly from its immediate neighbors and sometimes greatly from its remote neighbors. For instance, Indiana is not exactly like either Illinois or Ohio, but Indiana is vastly different from Oregon or Arizona. Kansas and Nebraska have a dozen minor differences, rather definitely marked, yet either is deeply different from Oklahoma, from California, or from Michigan. So we might go through the catalogue of western states charting differences—differences that would be deep in the matter of terrain, rainfall, vegetation, crops, industrial organization, so-called racial strains.

But when we have set down all the differences, the points of agreement would be found to be the really important points. And when we find those important points, the greatest common divisors of the states, we may be able to define roughly the essential qualities of that region in America known as the West. Politically it is agrarian—rural rather than urban. In only two or three states—Ohio, Illinois, possibly Michigan—do the great cities dominate the politics of their states. In all the other states, the farming areas and the small cities and towns dominate each state. Farmers and country-town statesmen in the West say what state taxes shall be levied and how the tax shall be spent. Merchants, stocking their counters, buy largely in the West for people on farms and in country towns. "Politics in business" in the West, barring eight or ten cities, are the "politics in business" of the farmer and the small townsman. The exceptions are Cincinnati, Cleveland, Detroit, Chicago, the Twin Cities, St. Louis, Kansas City, Denver, Seattle, Portland, San Francisco, and Los Angeles. The population of the West outside of these few industrial centers, and, indeed, in the various cities themselves outside of the small tenement area, is largely American-born of American-born parents. And again, outside of the ten or a dozen cities, the population is American-born of American-born grandparents. And to a large extent our western population springs from what is called the old American stock, English, Scotch, Irish, German, and Scandinavian citizens who have been in the country for half a century or more.

Populations from the ghettos of southern and central Europe are negligible in the West. The West is curiously overwhelmingly Protestant in religion. No

THE WEST THAT IS

one can doubt that religion does set the character of a people, or at least a dominant religious code or creed does reflect the dominant characteristics of any population. These western Protestants have given to the area a certain freedom and certain independence, which is shared by all other creeds. The western country has the Protestant virtues, which often go to seed and take the joy out of life: thrift, diligence, punctuality. But the West lacks and sorely needs the more distinctively Catholic qualities, a love of beauty, a sense of reverence, a capacity for faith in authority, that yearning for perfection which develops sainthood. On the other hand the Protestantism of the West is frankly a spiritual religion. It erects no physical symbols to incarnate its aspirations. It rejects physical miracles. Its prayers do not ask for fertility of fields or folds, and even in days or in places of drouth Protestant prayers for rain are shamefaced and generally are esteemed ridiculous. Indeed, this western Protestantism, although a descendant of New England Puritanism, is almost crassly, certainly militantly, a religion of the spirit, a spiritual religion with a God quite outside the material universe. The Protestantism which colors slightly all creeds in the West concerns itself with faith and morals which affect conduct, and after that concerns itself with little else. As pure Protestantism, it is founded upon a tolerant liberalism that never entirely surrendered, for instance, to the Ku Klux Klan.*

* Only in one western state, Indiana, did the Klan ever control state politics—considering Oklahoma more southern than western.

It is important to know how the Protestantism of this western country has been changed and modified by social growth and economic prosperity. The framework of Protestantism in the West, as expressed in the formal creeds of the more prosperous and powerful denominations—the Methodists, the Presbyterians, Alexander Campbell's Christians, the Baptists, the Congregationalists, the Episcopalians, and other subdivisions—has changed but little. A man's Protestant approach to God is direct. A free, unguided conscience still is the Protestant's only guide. The Protestant theology holds its plan of salvation as it was when the first tidal wave of immigration poured westward down the Allegheny slopes into the Ohio Valley. It is Milton's story: God was angry at the world for its sins. He sent Jesus his only begotten son, conceived for virgin birth in Mary, the wife of Joseph. Jesus came to the earth, preached repentance and righteousness, suffered on the Cross for the sins of the world, and so saved the world from God's just wrath and destruction. By accepting the sacrifice of Jesus the individual Protestant secures his salvation and place in heaven at the right hand of the Throne of God. According to Protestant theology he who rejects that salvation which came through the atonement of Jesus for the sins of the world when he dies in sin turns to the left without a purgatorial pause where there is "weeping and wailing and gnashing of teeth." That is the stark framework of the Protestant creedal theology.

The social salvation of humanity under Protestantism has come indirectly. As the individual has accepted salvation from the Christ, he has listened to Jesus' teaching. That teaching, largely founded upon the altruism of the Golden Rule, has remade men by enlarging their sense of duty. So as men have grown in a sense of duty they have recast their theory of civilization. Men sought heaven for their immortal souls through the acceptance of salvation. But converted sinners were taught and in some measure were directed and channeled by public opinion into lives of good will, humility, honesty and dutiful gracious neighborly kindness. In turn these Protestants being remade spiritually have erected public institutions in government which have ameliorated the hard lives of the poor. Moreover they have set up reason as the final arbiter in the relations of man. Out of this establishment of government and the social order upon reason rather than force, men have come into democracy. Incidentally they came to live under hard conditions of pioneer life as altruistic optimists in some semblance—even if remote at times—of neighborly association in the ideal of brotherly love. Men in the pioneer West have had to be hardworking to clear off the wilderness. They have had to be thrifty if they survived the economic rigors of pioneering. They have had to be punctual if they got on with their busy neighbors. They have had to be debt payers or fail. They have had to cultivate a rather strict sense of social duty. In other words the western Protestantism carried over the Puritan virtues into the continental West. All these hard virtues, all these social ideals, all these yearnings for the establishment of justice after debate and under reason, erected a social order wherein each individual came to rely with easy confidence upon the guidance of his conscience. In that order the noble life of Jesus and the gracious precepts of his philosophy set the pattern for individual conduct without mediator or priest. The Christian virtues and ideals impressed themselves upon the religionist. In the end, the plan of salvation, the theological framework of Protestantism, finally became secondary. Often theology was neglected. Sometimes the plan of salvation was almost forgotten by the communities established around the little white church.

Children in the public schools in the middle of the nineteenth century sang "Gospel hymns" on the opening of school, morning and afternoon. The "Gospel hymns" generally were not heavily complicated with theology. Generally they concerned themselves only a little about getting into heaven or keeping out of hell. That ecclesiastical unconcern about heaven or hell proved ultimately the weakness of the Protestant churches. But these songs taught the school children by ten thousand iterations the homely Puritan virtues —let us say the Christian virtues—those virtues which Paul, writing to the Galatians, called "the fruit of the Spirit," meaning specifically, "love, joy, peace, long-suffering, gentleness, goodness, faith, meekness, temperance." Which is another way of saying that the generation of the first decades of the nineteenth century taught to the children of the generation that came in the heart of the nineteenth century, the middle-class Protestant Puritan virtues which had sufficed the earlier generation as it came plunging into the eastern

THE WEST THAT IS

Mississippi Valley. The children born in the fifties, sixties, and seventies accepted Paul's schedule of virtues, and out of those virtues built the trans-Mississippi civilization. It is difficult to say whether the lives of these middle-class modern Puritans of the last quarter of the nineteenth century were cast out of the virtues which their fathers taught them in song and story, or whether the lives they were to lead, rather than the songs they sang, continued the influence of the precepts which had come into their youth. Probably their lives made their minds, middle-class minds, middle-class lives, Puritan, Protestant, nurtured upon "the fruit of the Spirit." Shakespeare had that middle class mind, and out of his life he enumerated the kingly graces thus: "justice, verity, temperance, stableness, bounty, perseverance, mercy, lowliness, devotion, patience, courage, fortitude." Which kingly virtues merely were the ideal moral reflex of the young yeoman Poacher of Avon building kings in his fancy. The play was from Jesus to Paul to Shakespeare and thence to the little white church and finally to the little red schoolhouse. In any case, the priest or the preacher had only a secondary place in the religious life of the West. Now for the songs that inspired the youthful hearts of our western grandfathers.

Pull for the shore, sailor, pull for the shore!
Heed not the rolling waves, but bend to the oar,
Safe in the lifeboat, sailor, cling to self no more,
Leave the poor old stranded wreck, and pull for the
    shore.

Here is little to strengthen a church promising the glory of heaven or the fear of hell-fire; but much to strengthen a state needing courageous purpose in its citizens. This song taught the children faith that man is good. From this song they learned the theory of spiritual regeneration which translated into common homely psychology means that every man is entitled to another chance.

Then the school children sang lustily another song, "The Ninety and Nine," which taught them mercy and compassion. It went:

> There were ninety and nine that safely lay
>   In the shelter of the fold,
> But one was out on the hills away
>   Far off from the gates of gold—
> Away on the mountains, wild and bare,
> Away from the tender Shepherd's care.

And often they sang about the "gate" that was "ajar" revealing the radiant Cross and the Savior's love. With what lusty exuberance they used to throw their heads back and sing:

> Oh, depth of mercy! can it be
> That gate was left ajar for me?
> For me, for me? Was left ajar for me?

The whole compassionate social program that rose in the states that were hewed out of the Western Em-

THE WEST THAT IS

pire—the social program from free schools to workingmen's compensation, from the universal ballot to the initiative and referendum—was implied in the mercy-loving democracy of these "Gospel hymns," that often lifted the roof of the little red schoolhouse and every Sunday waked the echoes around the little white church. The lesson of that mercy song was the dignity of the human spirit. It was the gospel of a fraternal equality—the subconscious footing stones beneath the political foundation of democracy.

> Work, for the night is coming,
>   Work through the morning hours;
> Work, while the dew is sparkling,
>   Work 'mid springing flowers.

Here the children, closing their eyes in musical ecstasy and opening their spirits to propaganda, learned diligence. They learned that the idler was to be scorned. Or they sang:

> "Hold the fort, for I am coming,"
>   Jesus signals still.
> Wave the answer back to Heaven,
>   "By Thy grace we will."

There was a rouser that poured courage into the childish soul as the public school pupils sat on their pioneer benches in the days of the frontier. Here is another:

> Let the lower lights be burning!
> Send a gleam across the wave!
> Some poor fainting, struggling seaman
> You may rescue, you may save.

In that song the children learned pity and a love for the underdog, certainly Christian virtues if there are any. Later after the Indians were all disposed of, that pity appeared in the fraternal folkways of the West. For when a child sings songs like these during his school years from six to sixteen, he is swallowing propaganda in large doses. Then the children sang also:

> Just as I am, without one plea,
> But that Thy blood was shed for me,
> And that Thou bid'st me come to Thee,
> O Lamb of God! I come, I come.

Here rhyme and rhythm and melody poured ideals of an aspiring humanity into their hearts. As they sang they learned that simplicity, that self-effacement, that self-examination which makes for "the pure in heart." And when they sang:

> I need Thee every hour,
>   Most gracious Lord;
> No tender voice like Thine,
>   Can peace afford.
> I need Thee, oh! I need Thee;
> Every hour I need Thee.
> O bless me now, my Savior,
> I come to Thee

THE WEST THAT IS

they were anchoring their consciousness to a Jesus who was gentle, kind, and loving, to a pattern of life that softens men and makes them more than kind. That song was an exercise in the imitation of the Christ. Little there was in these songs about the plan of salvation, the blood atonement and the heavenly rewards of the pious. In the churches also the hymnals were sometimes almost Buddhist in their emphasis upon the merging of the human spirit into the Nirvana, before the hymnals were revised in the latter part of the nineteenth century. "Rock of Ages, cleft for me, let me hide myself in Thee" might have been sung by a follower of Buddha in India. Another song,

> Soul of mine, in earthly temple,
> Why not here content abide?
> Why art thou forever pleading?
> Why art thou not satisfied?

celebrated the oneness of the universal spirit. In the chorus the seeker of truth cried out:

> I shall be satisfied, I shall be satisfied,
> When I awake in His likeness.

The hymnology of the pioneers, of course, gradually changed with the broadening of human enlightenment. The children with their "Gospel hymns" in the middle of the nineteenth century had come a long way from the hymns of their fathers, which came over from the colonial days:

> Remember, Lord, my dying cry!
> O Lord, remember me.

Or this lilting hymn of the camp meetings of Kentucky and Ohio on the western border in the early part of the nineteenth century, which gave sweet sensual surcease to the sinking spirit:

> In the arms of my dear Savior,
> Oh, there are ten thousand charms.

But these hymns and the reading of the New Testament, the Sermon on the Mount, the Beatitudes, the Parables in public schools without comment certainly did much to shape the character and, through the character, the destiny of the western citizenry in those days of the great westward trek of the American people. The "Gospel hymns" and the Bible reading sowed the seeds of an almost universal Protestantism in the soil of the new lands. The individual was exalted. His "free will," his independent spirit was nurtured on every side. With the western Protestant, life was a battle with sin. He had no confessional save "testimony" at camp meeting to soothe his soul and ease the struggle. Life was struggle. In that it was not unlike life on the "stern and rock bound coast" of another day and time. The Puritan of the prairie inherited his spiritual kingdom from the Puritan who lived among "Thy rocks and rills, Thy woods and templed hills" of New England and the lands of William Penn and the Dutch burghers. Of course as the environment of the westward-moving pioneer began to be softened, after the Indians were pushed into reservations, when machinery came to lighten the labors of man, when the increment of the soil began to form a cushion for the pioneers and their sons and grandsons, their religion reflected the easier, gentler life.

Of course this battle with sin which marked the religious life of the pioneer Protestant Puritans of the West did not always line up the forces of good against the powers of evil. Often what seemed to be the triumph of moral issues in western politics or in social controversies, later developed into the defense of folly or the defeat of ultimate wisdom. Sometimes the cohorts of Satan in the retrospect of a generation or two turned out to be champions of right. The angels of light often in the sun of another day proved to be sadly fanatical and miserably deluded. But nevertheless, as the propaganda for the primal virtues of courage, honesty, charity, and intelligence continued under the aegis of the church through the generations, the middle class became the ruling class: its mind, tempered by comforts and luxuries, stressed and to an extent energized into something like reality the middle-class Protestant virtues. Lives enjoying most of the fruits of the economic system set up by the increment of the land multiplied ten thousand fold by expanded credit, these lives set the standards of the times. These lives established the philosophy of the era. These lives defined beauty, wisdom, truth, mercy, peace, and justice in terms of the contemporary verities of the Protestant middle class in the western America of the nineteenth century. Thus from the ashes of the pioneers' campfires their cities arose. And out of their lives their minds were formed. So the social creed of the West bloomed, and its philosophy came to fruit. To know the West of today it is necessary to understand the West of yesterday. Its religion, its formal, ethical propaganda was more important than that of the West of today. But, for all that, today was erected upon yesterday out West.

A Democratic Trial Balance

Today in the West, the children no longer sing the "Gospel hymns" in the schools. Today in most churches, the emphasis in creeds is no longer upon theological differences. The plan of salvation, which was so important in the eighteenth century, here in the twentieth is a submerged and hidden reinforcement in the structure of Christian life. Certain ancient religious formulae persist, but atrophied. In the West one rarely hears hell-fire preached in a church large enough to support a pipe organ. The harp, the crown, and the long white robe of heaven have all but disappeared from sermons in the more prosperous churches of the West. The spirit of western Protestantism is an optimistic dualistic religion rendering unto God the things that are God's (that is, things of the spirit to be worshiped in the spirit), and unto Caesar this Protestantism of the West renders the things that are Caesar's (that is to say, the material world, its blessings and its calamities). Generally

THE WEST THAT IS

speaking in western Protestant America, heaven and hell as rewards and punishments have disappeared, except among the lower-income groups. When life becomes so hard that it does not justify itself, then a heaven is needed by the underprivileged and unfortunate to round out their ideals of justice. Then also hell is needed to punish those whom the oppressed, the baffled, and the futile have come to regard as their wicked enemies! So the fact that our hell has cooled and our heaven has lost its tinsel indicates that we have done well in a material way out here in the West, in the Protestant area, in the Bible belt if you will, even in the revised version of the Bible belt to be exact. Still abiding in a defensible triumph are that little red schoolhouse and that little white church upon which the ideals of the West have rested for a hundred and fifty years.

But let us not forget that in the United States we have an acquisitive civilization. Democratic capitalism merely furnishes a battlefield for the two warring instincts of man, his altruistic yearnings and his acquisitive instincts. And in the hundred and fifty years during which the West was settled, the influence of the church wrestled daily with the vast opportunities which the pioneer era offered to make money, to accumulate wealth by sharp practice and often by vicious devices. The history of this century and a half is full of national scandals. Great names were smirched. Every decade saw its major swindle. And as the real wealth and fluid capital of the pioneer West came out of the land, so swindlers operated on the land and the products of the land. The railroads, the coal mines, oil, the forests, all were exploited, all were used as media for swindling investors and for piling up dirty millions for unsocial men. Every state had its crooked land company. The school lands in many of the states were sold for a few cents an acre. The public lands were looted by corporations that hired men to take up bogus claims and sell them to organized promoters who in turn swindled investors.

When they grew up, those little children who sang the pious homilies in the schools and churches had a hard time keeping up with the scoundrels or joining the brigands who were out for loot. These social vandals, like the camp followers of a great army, plundered and robbed and poisoned the advancing columns of democracy as they marched across the continent.

Yet the boiled down essence of it in the final assessment and award of praise and blame at the end of a century and a half was good. The guerrillas that preyed upon the outposts and the rear guard of the army of democracy did not win the battle. Perhaps men would have built a better and nobler civilization if the acquisitive forces of humanity had been abolished. No one knows what would have happened if a swarm of angels had flocked across this continent. But this much is true: The civilization of our North American West was a better, a more equitable, a brighter human achievement than any other contemporary exodus of men in that century and a half. Not Africa, North or South America, nor Australia has so much to show at the end of the century and a half where the white man has conquered the wilderness as the pioneers of the western United States can show. Perhaps our North American continent was richer in soil, in forests, in mines than the lands where other white men trekked in those contemporary years. But certainly the American brand of democracy, for whatever reason may be assigned, did erect a civilization which is comparable with that of any other civilization which man set up in the last quarter of the eighteenth century and the hundred years that followed. The struggle between the two forces in the heart of man—his yearning to be neighborly and his instinct to grab and to hold—showed a fine score on this continent when the scores of other civilizations are seen. It is not necessary to mitigate and smooth over the evil that men did in those days. Set it all down, black as it was and is, beside the white to which men aspired, and the American gray is a lighter gray than that of any other pioneers in the wilderness of this world in the nineteenth century.

The Rule of the Middle Class

And because life in the main in this western country today is fairly decently adjusted, because on the whole among at least 60 per cent of the people the necessities of life are universal, the comforts of life are common, and the luxuries of life are not far beyond reach, we have a passably democratic civilization. It is deeply attached to what, for want of a better definition, we have come to call capitalism. It is democracy, capitalism, and Christendom, one in three and the three in one. And for short, let us call the trinity the American Middle Class.

The West is profoundly middle-class—probably more so than either the East or the South. For the South still holds vestigial ideals of a feudal aristocratic civilization and the great proletarian colored minority still is a part of the southern social organization. In the East, the financial centers of Philadelphia, New York, and Boston tend to build up a class-conscious ruling plutocracy on the right. On the left, in the mill towns and in the great industrial circles, hard times and rough living combine to establish and maintain a class-conscious proletariat. It is not large. But in the industrial East this class-conscious group of workers is sometimes vocal and always potentially dangerous to the middle class.

West of the Alleghenies, this line-up of a class-conscious group of rulers struggling with a class-conscious group of industrial workers exists in only four states —Ohio, Michigan, Illinois, and California. Only in Illinois and Michigan does the plutocracy organize itself so well that it tends to rule. But outside of the few cities of a million and more in the West, the social, economic, and political forces that dominate the western land are middle-class. Thus, speaking broadly and yet rather definitely, it may be affirmed safely not only that the West is middle-class, but that it is the American stronghold of the middle class. There in business, the small business man dominates the councils. In western politics, the congressmen who come to Washington and the minor statesmen who swarm

THE WEST THAT IS

through the capitols of the West, thinking in middle-class terms, work out laws and policies which will promote middle-class security. This middle-class solidarity of the West tends to give the West control of the country. For except in the matter of industrial problems, these middle-class westerners in the past have taken and held political leadership in Washington all out of proportion to the population or wealth of their states. These middle-class western leaders of opinion are, of course, liberal but rarely radical.

Middle-class ideals constantly encourage national policies which will obliterate the lines between the worker and the small business man. The middle class would fight the dictatorship of the proletariat by wiping out the proletariat and giving the worker the wages and living conditions which would admit him into the middle class. By the same token, the middle class would wipe out the plutocracy by redefining business honesty so that unconscionable profits would be curtailed and unscrupulous profiteers could not thrive and build up a plutocracy. This attitude toward the upper crust on one hand and what on the other hand the British call the lower orders, has been fostered by a long line of western statesmen for eighty years. This western middle class likes to keep things moving, its plutocrats coming down, its proletariat coming up through the middle class, both ways. We, of the American middle class, everywhere are class-conscious only in our zeal to break down class-consciousness and to wipe out the reasons for class-consciousness above and below. But out West we have built a civilization which in some approximation is realizing our ideals. We would instinctively make the middle class easy to enter from the bottom; hard to get out of from the top!

Obviously we of the West still are trying to restore that democratic relation, that neighborly mutual self-help which was the source of power for democracy in that West which was settled after the adoption of the American Constitution. We are also trying to give the little red schoolhouse its chance in so far as it symbolizes the advancement of knowledge and the practical use of knowledge in ameliorating the conditions of our life. Which, being translated roughly, means free enterprise where it remains honest enterprise. And there is the rub. In the definition of honesty in business, particularly in business of inordinate size, we of the western middle class come to clash with the forces of egoism, the centripetal forces that tend to hold special privileges and defy government to break them down. The overwhelming force of public opinion of that middle-class Protestant solidarity which we know as the West, is felt today and probably will be felt during this generation supporting any party or backing up any leader who will try by any measure to break down the power of our plutocracy. On the other hand we shall support parties, leaders, or measures that will clear away the barriers which tend to establish a proletariat. And remember this: These twenty-four states send half of all the Senators to the United States Senate. These western Senators vote their regional middle-class liberalism just as the Senators from the South and from the East vote for their regional interests. Also, don't forget that the South and the East are two sections, and all the West with half the United States Senators is only one. Western middle-class liberalism, which functions politically as easily in one party as in the other, is the strongest single political force in the United States for, more surely than either the East or the South, the West controls the United States Senate.

Panorama from the Air

Let me try to give you a picture of this West as it is today. Going over it in an airplane from Pittsburgh to Los Angeles, we see for nearly a thousand miles a vast checkerboard of farms. The section line which the surveyors drew straight as an arrow north and south, east and west in the wide area from Pittsburgh to the Rocky Mountains, seems to divide this great farming country into little rectangles. The lines of the rectangles are roads—township roads, county roads, state roads, national highways. These roads represent a fabulous investment as they have been improved in the last two decades. The township and county roads are covered with sand, macadam and gravel, the state roads with a bituminous mat, and many of the national highways are covered with a concrete slab. This road improvement, which has cost prodigal millions, has been necessary. Otherwise the people of the West would rattle the rivets out of their motorcars on the old-fashioned roads. Looking down from the airplane we see these little tin auto-bugs darting everywhere.

For the distribution of automobiles and trucks in this Mississippi Valley area allots one car to each family. Between the roads of this great alluvial valley north of the Ohio and the Red River, lie the farms. Within a small area around the great cities and the large industrial towns, the farms are truck farms, small, intensively cultivated. But most of the farms one sees in the first few hours of the flight westward are home farms, perhaps a hundred acres to two hundred acres in extent. They are marked off into small fields and pastures. A decent house rises on each farm surrounded by half a dozen well kept barns and outbuildings. In the last two or three years the house and a few of the outbuildings have been repainted. A bluegrass lawn, shade trees, and ornamental shrubs lie across and over the farmer's dooryard.

A unique thing about the West which one may not see from the airplane is the county line. Generally it is marked with a road—a county or a township road. The word "county" has its own meaning in the West. It is the political body which, generally by direct election, employs the sheriff, the prosecuting attorney, the recording officers, register of deeds, county clerk, the tax collectors and the administrative officers of the county known as the county commissioners. The county is generally twenty by twenty-five miles in extent. Going west of the Mississippi, the counties range larger than that. But from the airplane, as one travels west, one sees the little Ohio and Mississippi Valley towns dotted almost as regularly, on the landscape—though, of course, farther apart—as the farms

THE WEST THAT IS

and barns. These little towns in population from fifteen hundred to a hundred thousand are county-seat towns. They are not cities, but definitely country towns. Smaller communities—villages in each county—grow up in the various counties, six or a dozen miles from the county seat. The villages hold from three hundred to two thousand inhabitants.

In addition to the county lines are the township lines, fairly regular crisscross lines, from five to seven miles apart, north and south, east and west. These lines are township roads—the farm-to-market roads.

This rural county of the Mississippi Valley and the lake region is a unique division of the West. It derives from New England, Pennsylvania, and New York. But it is modified and becomes its own kind of political unit. Self-government which fifty years ago in the West tended to emphasize the township now tends to concentrate in the county. The local constable of the village and the township and the local justice of the peace are losing their power and authority to the sheriff and the district judge. The collapse of distance in the West is consolidating local government in the county seat.

As we pass over this western scene, just beyond the Alleghenies we cross an area approximately six hundred miles long, three hundred miles wide, a relatively small area of insignificant importance compared with the whole western Empire. In this narrow belt smoke stains the skies. Here are the industrial cities of Ohio (for instance, Cleveland, Dayton, Youngstown, and Cincinnati), the automobile factories of Michigan (Detroit and Flint), and the manufacturing towns of Indiana. At the western edge of the smoke-stained skies are the dingy industrial communities of urban Illinois with Chicago daubed in their midst around Lake Michigan. Outside that zone from Pittsburgh to Chicago, the other urban centers are set far apart among fields and pastures. The Twin Cities of Minnesota, Kansas City and St. Louis in Missouri, Denver in Colorado, and Omaha in Nebraska are hundreds of miles apart. Thus the westward-moving airplane gives an accurate estimate of the relation of the small urban population to the whole agrarian Mississippi Valley. For it is really a land of farms and country towns. But we do not see from the sky-view the unkempt character of the country—its winding weedy roadsides, its tenant farms going to rack and ruin, its shabby ramshackle town neighborhoods on the wrong side of the railroad track, its deepening ravines and widening gullies, its thinning topsoil, its abandoned rural schoolhouses, its scabby overpastured meadows—all evidences of social and economic decay. Of course, these evidences of change and decay do not dominate the scene. But they do threaten it.

If we ground the plane at any county-seat town from Ohio to western Kansas, north and south in this region, and walk along its streets, we shall find a typical community. First of all, the county-seat towns and the villages are covered with trees, elm trees south of Chicago and Cleveland, maple, oak and elm farther north. These shade trees almost hide the town

THE WEST THAT IS

from the aerial traveler. But nine months in the year they furnish long, cool Gothic green arches under which the town's motorcars flash up and down the paved highways. Westerners are losing their legs. They walk less and less. Beside the pavements which checker the western cities somewhat exactly, for crooked streets are almost unknown here, range the wide bluegrass lawns, always a little bit disheveled in July and August. Under the trees and in the lawns are separate houses (wooden houses for the most part), bordered by flowering shrubs and adorned with gardens where a procession of seasonal flowers blooms from March to late October. In every town is a dingy section, often obviously the abandoned residence section of a decayed and departed gentility. There live the poor. If a small industry or two raises its chimneys around the town, near the industry will be found the little houses of the industrial workers—sometimes well kept, more often seedy and disheveled. But against the defects in the picture the visitor will find that nearly every town will have its public library, its stadium, its town hall. The business section of a county-seat town of five to fifty thousand people generally consists of a few streets, three or four thousand feet in extent, fairly well in the center of the town. Generally two or three buildings, from five to a dozen stories, which house the bank and the offices of the doctors and the lawyers, are the architectural overlords of the business section. Throughout the town one finds groups of handsome temples. These are the schoolhouses, the lineal descendants of the little red schoolhouse that once stood beside the little white church of the pioneers. These schoolhouses are set in wide, well-kept lawns and indicate the expenditure of much money to keep them going. Among the trees in the residence section will be found many churches, probably a dozen for each ten thousand in the community. They are not so splendid in their architecture and appointments as the schoolhouses. In the last generation the little red schoolhouse has done rather better than the little white church. A hospital or two with a hundred beds each is likely to be found in these county seats. And at the edge of one out of a dozen of such towns a college rises. If it is a state institution, it represents an investment of several million dollars. If it is a denominational school, the half-dozen buildings probably could be reproduced for something like one million dollars. But every college is set among trees in a wide campus with a stadium of some sort at the edge of the campus, and students' motorcars stand parked all over the lot.

The stores in the business section are filled with every modern luxury. The movie palaces, gorgeous and rococo in their architecture in these western country towns, show pictures a few days after the New York or Hollywood releases. And in the windows of the dry-goods and clothing stores are New York's Fifth Avenue styles or Hollywood's latest designs not more than ten days old. In the food stores are assembled unbelievable quantities of exotic fruits and vegetables that have no season. These green groceries come daily on trucks and by rail from the South the

THE WEST THAT IS

year around. These exotic foods and this fashionable clothing are used by the 60 per cent of the townspeople who live in the well-kept houses, some of whom even live in the smart subdivisions with snappy, modern architecture more or less, if reduced to scale, like the palaces of Long Island. There is no western hinterland in food, in clothing, in houses.

This American middle class runs the same across the land. The one thing that marks the West is that there the middle class is larger than elsewhere. It dominates the scene. Its stores on Main Street, its tall office buildings, the doctors' and the lawyers' offices and business places of realtors and the traders, are built on one model, the urban model that prevails all over the country. In the residences radios prattle by the hour, mechanical babblers pouring out their idiocy unchecked and often unheeded. For the radio and the automobile are two modern machines that have transcended class lines. They tend to equalize the privileges of the plutocrat and the proletarian. The car, the telephone, and the radio are no longer marks of the middle class anywhere—except in great urban areas. The county-seat town of the Mississippi Valley goes to the farthest salient of democratic civilization in its comfort and in the distribution of its luxuries. Life is probably easier there for the common man, and opportunity probably more wide-open for his children than it is anywhere else on earth.

Passing out of town into the country in the West, the story is not so cheerful. Here too often are weeds. Here frequently thrift is missing. Tenantry is coming.

The Grade A farmer survives and is doing well. The Grade B farmer is struggling with debt. The Grade C farmer, who is now for the most part a tenant, is found too frequently. Moreover he is leaving the farm, and the miserable spectacle of the abandoned farm in the West is entirely too common for comfort. The ranks of the unemployed and those under direct relief in the farming area were swelling year by year during the fourth decade of this century. With all our tinkering and in the face of our noble aspiration for recovery, we have not begun to solve the problem of the farmer.

As for the dozen cities of the West, they are like all the cities of the continent. The distressed areas in these western towns and cities are obvious, and the best that can be done is to keep those areas from widening. The city problem is not a western problem. It is an American problem and touches the metropolitan areas of all the land. But the farm problem is essentially a western problem, the problem of the Mississippi Valley. To that we shall turn later. (In the South the farm program is grounded in cotton. And there it is somewhat a social problem!)

As one flies west across the Mississippi Valley, three to five hundred miles westward from the great river which divides the continent, one sees a change in the aspect of the land. In the trans-Mississippi country the farms checkered upon the board below the airplane, grow larger. Instead of the home farm with a hundred or two hundred acres, the farms five hundred miles or so beyond the Mississippi begin to widen to five hundred or a thousand, or ten thousand acres.

THE WEST THAT IS

The county-seat towns begin to run smaller. In population, they range from fifteen hundred to ten thousand. Something has happened that the airplane does not record. It is the rise in altitude of the land. We have left the prairies with their alluvial soil. We are now flying across the high plains over a loose sandy soil, as we approach within three or four hundred miles of the Rocky Mountains. Here, from western Oklahoma northward through western Kansas and western Nebraska across the western Dakotas to Canada is a one-crop country. The high plains lie at an altitude of from three to six thousand feet above sea-level. Here the valleys shrink. Here the rivers are sluggish, dry beds of sand from flood time in June to flood time the following May. But the little towns are just as bright and gay as they are in the alluvial section of the valley to the eastward. As many cars speed along the highways in proportion to the population as are found elsewhere in the West. But the one-crop land, the wheat land which in recent years has been turned back somewhat to grazing pastures, presents another economic set-up from that which we see as we cross the Mississippi Valley just westward from the Alleghenies. The high plains are of their own kind. No huge factories are here, few small industries. The school buildings are as gay and gaudy in these county-seat towns of the high plains as they are elsewhere. But the colleges are fewer and smaller. The trees are not so high on the plains and are harder to grow than they are farther to the east. This is a pastoral country. Abraham, out of the land of Ur with his herds, would have understood this wheat and pasture country better than he would have understood the civilization in the Ohio and the Great Lakes country. Plains people tend to live in towns and villages and farm by machinery. The great herds and the great wheat fields indicate that agriculture on the high plains is passing from a way of life to an industrial process.

As the plane lifts from five to ten thousand feet for the Rocky Mountains, one sees another type of American life. Here are the irrigated farms and the towns where smelters rise and stain the sky with their smoke. Here in the deep green valleys between the snow-covered ranges are fruit farms, vegetable farms, vast truck farms. Here water melting from the eternal snows sustains the life of the region. It was in such a place in another time that the Psalmist lived who cried: "I will lift up mine eyes unto the hills, from whence cometh my help." This Rocky Mountain region from central Colorado across the Sierras and the rich lovely land that slopes down to the Pacific Ocean is, of course, the West— the Far West. Like the West the mountain region is still middle class, still Protestant, still thrifty, and still of a rural rather than an urban civilization. Herds graze upon these rocky hills. Here are great wheat fields in these irrigated valleys. Here are mines and forests with their special industries. But it is all middle class, all country-town and agrarian, a part of the great West.

On the Pacific Coast we have still another region, but it remains the West. In the two northern states,

Washington and Oregon, industries are not unlike those of the Mountain states. The cities, Portland and Seattle, are not unlike the cities of the wide Mississippi Valley. But California is different. California is semitropical. California still is rural. Her largest city, Los Angeles, is a magnified country town. San Francisco is really urban, the only sophisticated city on our Pacific Coast. But in these three coastal states, for all the differences in climate, in rainfall, and in topography, the county remains a unit of government, the county seat is the center of culture, and man lives by tilling the soil. The problems of man on the Pacific Coast are agrarian problems. The West does not surrender to the climate or topography of the farthest western states.

Challenge to the Middle Class

Here then in this great region, from Buffalo to the Pacific, is a middle-class civilization politically devoted to old-fashioned liberalism as against the dour radicalism which might some day reform the United States by taking it to the totalitarian philosophy of state capitalism or which would erect another tyranny upon the dictatorship of the proletariat. In ordinary times, with the economy of democratic capitalism sailing in smooth waters, this middle-class liberalism of the West would not be in danger. This middle-class liberalism could take care of itself if left to itself. It could hold its present power, achieving necessary economic and political changes by the slow democratic evolutionary process in terms of decades and generations and, at most, of centuries. In all good time the American middle class could spread those blessings of life and the bounties that rise out of the growth of physical power through machinery to those who are underprivileged.

Given time, whatever increment may be developed from increased mechanical power could be distributed fairly equitably throughout the social body. For three decades in the twentieth century after the West filled up, when the last state was enclosed in its boundaries, after the last railroad spike was driven, and the last boom city was established, this western-bred liberalism sufficed. The middle class thrived. Democracy functioned not, of course, in perfection, but American opportunity at least in the West was kept open so that the poor man's children could rise to the full enjoyment of the civilization which was based somewhat upon the poor man's wrongs. Discontent was minimized in those first three decades of our century by an ascending spiral of prosperity. In the prosperity of the years from Grover Cleveland to Franklin Roosevelt, in the West, at least, social and economic forces managed to keep something like social justice on the economic assembly line moving up from the lower income groups into the middle income groups, while the biological law of inheritance kept pulling down from the social and economic top the dumb ones who accidentally were sheltered there by the exceptional capacities of their fathers. We did have, in that generation, democracy, still functioning at least in the great West where a little profit might be depended upon to channel into fluid capital and to convert into expanding credit, the incremented income from the rise in the price of land.

Our western democracy was not rampant. It was not unchallenged. But it survived and for all practical purposes democracy did its job, held its place, was not menaced. Speaking broadly, even now out West democracy is anchored in the hearts of the people. The anchors are barnacled a little in the industrial centers. Agriculture has a real problem which in too many marginal cases is becoming acute. The dissatisfied industrial worker in Ohio, Michigan, Illinois, to a certain extent in Indiana, Minnesota, and California, and the discontented farmer all over the West, have set red danger signals blinking. It is not critical, this danger, but it is there. We find it easy to say, "Well, given good times, the trouble will all be over." But what are good times? Where are good times? Why are good times delayed? How long can these danger signals blink at us and not mean real danger? The number of marginal farmers is probably increasing. Unemployment even in the West is not perceptibly falling. For a catastrophic decade, western middle-class democracy founded upon the Christian ethic and grounded in capitalism has stood like a rock. But like a rock our democratic capitalism has forces beneath it which slowly are eating into a place where the rock may shift and veer if it does not tumble.

For we of the West today are in the midst of ominous challenging forces which come from afar. For the first time in American history middle-class liberalism is not entirely self-sufficient. The West, after all, is a part of the United States. And with the industrial East in serious distress, with the rural South staggering under its problems, the West, the liberal middle-class West, founded upon what we like to feel are democratic ideals plus the horse sense of the little white church and the little red schoolhouse of the pioneers, cannot minimize the symptoms of injustice and unrest. We cannot face tomorrow without the uneasy realization that the solid middle-class Protestant West, like all the world, is facing danger and change.

III

THE PECULIAR PROBLEM OF THE WEST

It is necessary here to pause for a moment, in telling the story of the West, and set down the dominant problem of the West—the farm problem. Three men may be distrusted who discuss the farm problem: first, the man who denies there is a problem; second, the man who declares that he can solve it by any formula, or that he can cure the farmer's many ills by one panacea; and third, he may be distrusted who says, "Let the farm problem ride." For it is a serious problem, rapidly becoming acute! Upon some solution of the farm problem rests the stability of our American institutions and the continuance of life on this continent under American ideals. We cannot tolerate a peasant class—for economic rather than moral reasons.

The United States faces many farm problems, each more or less unique in its way. For instance: the farm problems of the eastern coastal states north of the cotton belt are largely marketing problems, truck gardeners' problems, the problems of small farmers who are near a domestic market. And the farm problem south of the Mason and Dixon line is somewhat social, complicated by a tottering feudal system, a hang-over from the days of human slavery. The southern problem is a problem of cotton and tobacco and of the negro proletarians, of the poor whites, and of the fading gentry which together have set up a backward civilization.*

But the problem which concerns us here and now is a problem of its own kind in our western country. It arises largely out of the fact that western farmers (the farmers from Buffalo to Los Angeles, from Pittsburgh to Seattle) established in the nineteenth century and the first decade of this century their own way of life. They were the first farmer pioneers of any wide continental area who were not content to be peasants. They set up a scale of living under which, because they had votes, they created schools, built roads, established governmental services, and levied taxes far in advance of the living standards and government services enjoyed by other rural people in other lands. They paid for their high living standards somewhat (probably largely), out of the increment of the land. The father of a family of boys in the early nineteenth century was able to sell part of the land he had cleared, part of the farm he had opened, for a price high enough to establish all the boys on farms on the cheap land farther west; and they, in the middle of the nineteenth century, moved from the Ohio Valley into the

* By way of a solution of the southern farm problem, the federal government is doing two self-destructive things: trying to subsidize the tenant farmer so that he can buy land and break up the plantation system, and at the same time the federal government is trying to subsidize the price of cotton, making it so high that the planters can afford not to sell the land at a price the tenants can pay.

western Mississippi Valley—that is, into Wisconsin, Minnesota, and Iowa—and built their farms on cheap land which in turn increased in value so that they could establish their sons in Kansas, Nebraska, and the Dakotas. And the sons on the western prairies sent their sons to the irrigated land of the desert and the mountains. And with the increase in the price of the virgin soil of the prairies and of the mountain valleys, the sons of the sons of the sons of those who climbed over the Alleghenies and settled in Ohio and Indiana, went down the Sierras into California with enough surplus capital to establish a new, strange beautiful subtropical civilization in the coastal states facing the Pacific.

But when the last great-grandson of the pioneers had settled on the last free farm or opened the last cheap land, the American farm problem began to face the nation. From 1914, when the farmer's produce brought a price on a parity with the things the farmer needed for a comfortable life, farming has had to stand on its own resources. And obviously farming cannot stand alone. Only a farmer whose farm is a self-sufficient unit can go it alone. That farmer has gone. The western farmer now must rise or fall upon the purchasing power of the industrial worker.

During the first decade of the new century, the balance between the prices which the farmer received for his produce and the prices which he paid for his necessities and comforts was fairly even. The year 1914 is classically established as a year of parity for the farmer. He was doing fairly well then. The farm problem as a national economic problem was somewhat quiescent. The political Grangers and Greenbackers were a memory. The Farmers Alliance and the Populists had disappeared. The co-operative movement, if it had survived the 1890's, was all but negligible in the national economy; and the drift and tendency of world conditions seemed somehow to give the American farmer a reasonably advantageous position, at least a tolerable position, in our national life.

The World War, which immediately stimulated the demand for farm produce and so quickly raised the price thereof, made the farmer a gambler. His good times ruined him. He laid by no surplus after the manner of industrialists. It is easy to say that the farmer could not stand prosperity. It is obvious that he went in for a lot of luxuries which became comforts—the telephone, the motorcar, the movies, good roads, processed foods. These comfortable luxuries created wants, and wants created habits, and habits created an American way of rural life during the second decade of the twentieth century which again greatly lifted the farmer's standard of living. Also, incidentally his changed life changed his cast of thought. The war price of grain and of cattle seemed to justify store clothes, store foods, tractors, an eight-month school, all-weather roads, and a mortgage to buy, first the adjoining "eighty," and then the quarter-section adjoining that. All the world was wasting economic goods in war, wasting everything the farmer produced. His grain, his cattle, his cotton, his wool were fed into the insatiable maw of war and there were destroyed.

PECULIAR PROBLEM OF THE WEST 63

More than that, all that the miners dug from the earth, all that the men at the forge welded into industrial material, many of the machines to make machines, the capital goods of Christendom, were dumped into the hopper of war and destroyed. Thus everything the farmer did when he was not saving for a surplus between 1914 and 1918, when he was borrowing and spending, was a complete loss to the economy of the world. Spiritually he was stepping out, high, wide, and handsome, from the old way of farm life into a new way of thinking.

Little really was saved from the war boom. The farmer could not realize this any more than did the capitalist who backed the farmer and at the same time backed the industrialists. The capitalist had mortgaged his future in the hope of present profits. But the capitalist had a reserve, a reserve of credit rather than cash, while the farmer, alas, in those mad war days, built up no reserve. What he built up was debt, somewhat a gambling debt, to buy land at fantastic prices in the Mississippi Basin, for instance. He mortgaged his future in the hope of everlasting profits figured on the basis of those which came to him out of the unique and terrible economy of the war. So at the opening of the third decade the American farmer was up to his ears in debt. Gossip at the time declared that the deflation of the early 1920's was aimed at organized labor. But it really hit the American farmer. The real increment of land, the pioneer's source of fluid capital was gone. It was sunset for the Golden Age.

The farmer's debt was the basis of the farm problem of the twenties. The problem produced controlling political minorities—the modern term is "pressure groups"—in the upper Mississippi Valley. A congressional farm bloc was formed, potent chiefly in the Republican senatorial majority in the days of Harding, Coolidge, and Hoover. This farm bloc, united with the Democrats of the South in Congress, often made a majority in the United States Senate. Sometimes the farm bloc controlled majorities in the House of Representatives. At the beginning of the Coolidge elective term, these embattled farmers were able to hold up the election of a speaker of the national House of Representatives for several days. In the first decade of the century, the same group, then known as the "Insurgents" (but in the 1920's known as the "Progressives") overthrew Uncle Joe Cannon, the conservative Republican speaker of the House. Thirty years ago in 1909, only a conservative alliance between the regular Republicans of the industrial East and Tammany saved the remnants of the Republican House organization from annihilation. In Coolidge's day and in Hoover's, the Democrats were cannier. They either could not or would not rescue the conservative Republicans. So with the aid of canny Democrats the Mississippi Valley farmers took senatorial control from the last two Republican Presidents. This congressional independent bloc, organized loosely around the farm bloc, voted together on most political questions, some rather remote from the farm problem. But at base the discontent of the American farmer in the Mississippi Valley and in the Far West was the dominant force in the national politics of the third decade.

The Plowman Plods His Weary Way!

The American farmer in that day was trying to get the American price of American farm products so adjusted that he could afford to buy what he felt were the basic needs of a self-respecting citizen of the United States. The farmer in this country always has refused the peasant's economic status. The fact that as an American citizen he could use his ballot effectively to control state legislatures and the Congress within his party, gave him a sense of power, a self-reliant dignity which made him feel his essential equality with the capitalist and the industrial worker. He had that vast sense of self-respect which inflated the ego of his pioneer grandfather who squinted at life through a rifle sight. If the factory workers had silk shirts in the 1920's, along with automobiles, movies, and radios, high schools for their children, telephones and electric appliances in their lives—well enough; but the farmer also demanded them. The farmer required permanent, all-weather roads for his new motorcar and for his marketing truck. Then tractors came to the western Mississippi farm during the war. The "combine," a machine which cut and threshed the wheat farmer's grain in one operation, also came to the farm on the high plains. The farmer had increased his budget with new farm machinery, with taxes for good roads, with seven-month or eight-month schools and rural high schools, with telephone bills, and with money for the movies in every little town of the Mississippi Valley within five or six miles from every farm. Thus one sees why the American farmer who also was a gambler in land during the World War had his unique problem; why he felt put upon; why he went into politics in the fourth decade with blood in his eye. He was asking only what the small-town merchant, the railroad laborer, the country doctor, the courthouse politician, the city schoolteacher were asking of life—and getting. They could afford what the farmer demanded. But the townsmen did not have a self-sufficient economy—an ancient way of life—which in many cases was possible to the forehanded farmer. He refused to subtract that sufficiency from his other demands. He expected that way of life in addition to those delightful comforts and luxuries which he had taken to the farm immediately after the war.

The income from his grain and hay crops, from his cattle and hogs, from chickens and sheep and pigs, did not let him live in the style to which he had become accustomed. He felt that his new life was his royal American birthright. So through the third decade in the Administrations of Harding, of Coolidge, and of Hoover, the farmer produced a problem in our politics by creating an intransigent congressional minority which took away the power and the glory of the major party and made the President more or less a suppliant to leaders of the farm bloc. The Progressives, a party in a party, which dominated the farm bloc, were

PECULIAR PROBLEM OF THE WEST

led by the elder La Follette and his sons, by the Senators of the western Missouri Valley and by their congressional neighbors from the Missouri and Arkansas rivers to the west coast. Southern Democrats, partly promoting party strategy to weaken the Republicans, but largely because the South is rural and not industrial, joined with these Mississippi Valley Progressives, and all hands tinkered with the farm problem.

During this prosperous third decade, the time of the big bull market, starting after the currency deflation a few years before, from the middle twenties until the beginning of the thirties, the western farmer angrily felt that his purchasing power was curtailed. The fixed charges in interest on his old debt (the debt of the war days) and his rising taxes for improved schools, for good roads, and for the new services of government (public health, road patrol, state welfare legislation, and the extension of governmental authority over utilities corporations) were cutting down his surplus income.

But the western American farmer saw no reason why he should not have these things if the townsman of moderate means and income had them. So various price-fixing schemes to pay for expanded rural life appeared as legislative measures before the committees of Congress. The McNary-Haugen bill passed Congress with the votes of the South and the West. President Coolidge vetoed it, with an accolade of approval from New England and the north Atlantic coast. But he approved a national agency for making farm loans at cheap interest. President Hoover yielded to the demand for price fixing, bought wheat to stabilize the price of wheat; and every bushel placed in storage virtually remained upon the market. The price of wheat, therefore, went down instead of up. Europe was teetering to its financial debacle. The new tariff bill had shut off American imports. The outside world could not buy the farmer's produce, and forty-cent wheat and two-bit corn came to the American market. President Hoover unjustly paid the price of yielding to the demands of the farmers. The price of livestock went down. Pigs and chickens lost their value. Millions of workers were walking the streets looking for jobs during the last years of the Hoover administration—somewhat because, at the farmer's own demand for price fixing, the farmer's buying power was cut down. Industry was dead. Even the farmer's home market was gone. The descending economic spiral whirled America to calamity. In desperation the American farmer—normally a Republican except in the South—turned in 1932 to Franklin Roosevelt.

President Roosevelt in 1932 carried the Congress with him. Also with him went many statehouses in the normally Republican Mississippi Valley and in New England, but not the county courthouses—important politically west of the Alleghenies. Apparently the western farmer was voting his suspicions nationally, from '30 to '38, and his real convictions locally. He did not change his party politics, but the western farmer suspected that nationally his party was in league

PECULIAR PROBLEM OF THE WEST

with the forces which he felt were destroying him, notably by the tariff. He was also more than suspicious; he was definitely hostile to that vague community of commercial, financial, and industrial interests which in his mind he lumped into the phrase "big business" —"Wall Street" of the Grangers, Greenbackers, and Populists. Also little business irked the farmer, the local Chamber of Commerce as much as Wall Street, in those years of the collapse of the stock market and the depression of all prices. For many a local Chamber of Commerce in the twenties had joined with the national Chamber of Commerce in denouncing all legislative farm programs offered by the farm leaders in their various organizations. The programs included the McNary-Haugen bill under Coolidge, and the federal farm loan banks, as well as farm price fixing under Hoover. So the farmer nationally turned to the New Deal. But locally he stood pat.

Roosevelt Opens Pandora's Box

When Franklin Roosevelt began to realize, in the second or third year of his first term, that he was facing at least half a dozen, probably half a score, of distinctly different farm problems, he and his advisers began to see that simplification was no longer a possible solution of the western farm problem. Then it may have become apparent, too, that even the fundamental terms of the farm problem produced a different problem in different localities. The word "wheat" in Ohio, Indiana, Illinois, Michigan, meant something entirely different from the word "wheat" used in western Texas, western Oklahoma, western Kansas, western Nebraska, Montana, and the Dakotas. Around the Great Lakes, farmers who grow wheat grow it in small fields, from twenty to two hundred acres. In the trans-Mississippi country, in the Missouri Valley, and in the valleys of the Arkansas and the Red River, the farmers of the high plain west of the hundredth meridian, grow wheat on farms ranging from one hundred to ten thousand acres. Wheat in the high plains is an industrial process. Wheat in the northern Ohio Valley is a problem that affects farming as a way of life. The farmer on the high plains just east of the Rockies, in a considerable minority of cases, does not live on his farm. He lives in the nearest county-seat town to his farm or in the nearest sizable little city. He plows the ground for his wheat with a tractor in August and sows it from a tractor in early September, goes away and lets it alone until his tractor brings his "combine" into the field nine months later. Then he reaps his crop —if he has one—and threshes it at one operation. If he gets three annual crops out of five he is prosperous. He can live on two crops out of five. He can raise wheat profitably at sixty cents a bushel. His land is cheap. Mass production cuts down his costs.

But three hours' motor journey eastward, the farmer with the family-sized farm cannot compete with the wheat industrialist in the high plains. Yet both are American citizens. Each has his rights, if either has the questionable right, to the benevolent protection and fraternal assistance of his government. In his own

PECULIAR PROBLEM OF THE WEST 71

way, the wheat farmer of the high plains is establishing his own social phase of the farm problem. The uncertain weather of the region makes rainfall precarious, and his whole business becomes a gamble. Moreover, the price of his wheat is affected by competition around the globe. A war in China, the threat of war in the Ukraine, a political upheaval in the Mediterranean, affects this wheat grower's price on the high plains of our West, and in the Rocky Mountain areas. There he has only one alternative crop—his short grass. He may be a stockman, but if he is a stockman his problem as a producer of meat is vastly different from that of the barnyard farmer who has a couple of "eighties" in tame grass, a dozen or fifty steers and a few dairy cattle. And again, the word "livestock" means one thing west of the hundredth meridian and through the Rocky Mountains and quite another thing from the Mississippi River east to the Atlantic Ocean.

Another diverting division in the terminology of the farm problem appears when we consider differences between crops grown under rainfall and crops grown under irrigation. In the mountain states, from Canada to Mexico, are millions of acres lying on what was once the Great American Desert; now they are watered by irrigation projects. Most of these irrigation projects are in one way or another subsidized by the government. The farms built up under the great dams of the region are no longer individual farms as farms are in the Mississippi Valley and in the seaboard states. These farms of the mountain region carry heavy charges for irrigation. The irrigated farms are more or less co-operative as they lie under one dam and pay tribute to one reclamation project or another—interest on bonds, for instance, and amortization.

There in the Far West the farmer is tied closely to his neighbors. The old pioneer who was his own master inside his own fence, the farmer who for three hundred years has refused to be a peasant and at the same time has refused to surrender his royal American independence, in the nature of things is a different farmer, with different problems, with a different spiritual outlook, with different industrial interests and social reactions from the irrigation farmer. Even the one-crop farmer of the high plains, like the farmer along the rich broad valleys of the streams that pour into the Mississippi from the west, is unique in his rural needs and social outlook. But these farmers, all of them—the truck gardeners of the seaboard, the small farmers of the eastern Mississippi Valley, the leaders of the feudal society of the South, the wheat barons and the cattle kings of the high plains of the Rockies, and, again, on the western slope of the Sierras, the citrus fruit growers of California—have their distinct farm problems.

The farmers in each region are working out their own farm lives. And the essential bewilderment of the farm problem comes from the fact that all of these farmers with all their problems put all their ballots into one box. All of them vote for one thing, federal aid for the American farmer—but federal aid means half a dozen different things.

Is it a wonder that honest statesmen grow gray, and

PECULIAR PROBLEM OF THE WEST 73

that Congressmen with little wisdom and a great desire for political survival turn demagogues? The very size of our country, with its multitude of interests within this one great calling, produces such a clamor of farm voices that it is seriously doubtful if one answer ever can quiet the uproar.

But no one can deny that the United States has a farm problem arising from many farm problems. For everywhere the American farm population is suffering from a mounting farm tenancy, growing farm debt, and, in the last ten years, the increasing number of mortgage foreclosures. The "Grade A" farmer is escaping many of the ills of his less competent brethren. But the successful farmer is the exception. His fellow farmer's name is legion; and the unmortgaged landowners who are "making a go of it" are not numerous enough to take as a criterion in considering the farmer. About the best the rest of us can do for the prosperous exception to the average distressed farmer is to let the farmer with ten talents alone, and not hamper him. Certainly the statistics of the last two decades indicate that agriculture is a crippled industry—we have the problem of the crippled farm common in every region of our land. And perhaps, indeed probably, the farm problem of the western farmer will be solved only when the purchasing power of the industrial worker is expanded. Of the eleven million unemployed, two or three million can never earn enough to fairly receive $3 a day. But the other eight million have a real economic wage value of $1,800 a year per man. Moreover, on the assembly belt dropping rivets, at least half of the dull ones can give real social return for the living wages. To put these idle men to work is one partial, perhaps major, solution of the farm problems.

And now let us turn our eyes upon one rural statesman, Senator Arthur Capper of Kansas, who in Coolidge's day and Hoover's was chairman of the farm bloc in the United States Senate. He makes no pretense to vast erudition, even about the farm problem. He lays no claim to be the farmer's rock in a weary land. He keeps his ear to the prairie grass and has but one proud boast: he doesn't let the bugs get in it. He is not a radical. He was a frequent house guest at the White House in Coolidge's day. President Hoover consulted him. He has the confidence and respect of President Roosevelt. He is trying, as a score or two of our western Senators are trying, to find some path, some royal road to the solution of this intricate, almost insoluble problem. In December, 1938, just before Congress met, Senator Capper asked the farmers of his own state to come to a conference with him. He issued a general call. He expected them to meet in the Rainbow Room of his hotel. He had four hundred chairs provided. Half an hour before the meeting, the chairs were filled. He adjourned the conference to a larger room, and then still a larger one, and twelve hundred farmers finally sat down in one of the public halls of Topeka while Senator Capper presided and listened to his farmer friends.

It was bedlam. Senator Capper's Kansas is divided exactly in the middle by the hundredth meridian. The wheat growers and the cattlemen of the high sandy

PECULIAR PROBLEM OF THE WEST

plains brought to the meeting their own solution of the farm problem. The barnyard cattleman, who is a subsistence farmer in the lower alluvial uplands and valleys—who has an "eighty" in wheat, forty acres in alfalfa, and a hundred of his second bottom acres in sorghum—this farmer with a little orchard and a garden plot and with lilacs on the bluegrass lawn, came with his problems. Then the owners of a few irrigated farms in the Arkansas River Valley, who grow sugar beets, came with their notions of the farm problem. Finally came the dairy farmer. He is increasing in strength and grace in Kansas, and he had an entirely different problem from his neighbor across the highway who is growing Hereford beef cattle.

The Tower of Babel was comparatively an a cappella choir, singing in perfect harmony, beside the Kansas Senator's farm conference. Capper is a mild man. In that meeting he tried to compromise differences. All day long he sat trying to soothe opposing groups, to bring them together. He refused to take sides. How could he? Each group was right according to its own lights and needs, and each group had interests deeply and diametrically opposed to at least one of the other groups. As the clamorous hours passed, these farmers gave no sign or signal of the least agreement. It was a cat fight. Senator Capper, patiently, sweetly, gently smiling, and withholding commitment to any section of the raucous uproar, sat through it all. At last one old Puritan from eastern Kansas, a barnyard stockman with half a dozen crops on his three hundred acres, rose up in exasperation and, shaking his finger at the Senator, cried, "Oh, Senator, we are all tired of seeing you so damn wishy-washy!" And for a minute, there was one gorgeous unanimity in the explosion of uproarious delight. Then they all realized that the Senator was not without courage. He was just without the wisdom of Solomon to take side or part in the interminable, uncompromisable, irrepressible conflicts of the hour.

It would seem that, more or less, the farm problem in the West is the product of the Pacific Ocean. If we could have had land thirty years ago, cheap fertile land for another thousand miles to the westward, from California, we might easily have relieved the pressure upon the American farmer that has come with the twentieth century. Some way with the increment in the price of that new land of the temperate zone, another generation would have distributed with the same democratic approximation of justice the increment in the rising value of that land; and the American farmer of the lake states, of the Mississippi Valley, of the desert, and the mountains of the Pacific slope might have found in the economic digestive processes his share of the rising land values coursing through the blood of our economic body. But the Pacific Ocean raised the bar.

Alas, Hawaii is the land of squatting labor. The Chinese and the Japanese once did, and the Filipinos now do, the work in the tropical fields which the white men will not do. The Philippine Islands offered the American farmer nothing, though the schoolteacher, the lawyer, the merchant, the manufacturer found outlets

PECULIAR PROBLEM OF THE WEST

there for their talents. So after the World War with its inflated prices and its abnormal economic status, the farm problem became acute.

The farm problem cannot ride along much further. The American farmer will not be a peasant. He has a ballot. He can read and write. He has gone to an eight-month school. Young farmers and their wives have been through high school and have known something of college. They will not be declassed. They have learned to organize politically. They have power of life and death over our politicians. More than that, in the farmer's hands, who has a balance of power between the parties, lies the decision of the way our country shall go, the economic and social course it will take during this century. This balance of power in the West is an actual majority in most western states. And as the West has half of the Senators of the United States and a dominant minority of the members of the House of Representatives, the farmer holds a national balance of power. The power of the farmer in American politics is responsible for the continual tinkering with the farm problem which has occupied much of the time and energy of the American Congress in the last two decades.

Politicians in both parties have been trying earnestly but honestly since the World War of the second decade to find some economic substitute for the rising price of land which kept the West afloat during the nineteenth century and the first decade of the twentieth. Time and again leaders have appeared with panaceas which would grant a bonus to the farmer concealed or unconcealed—this bonus was expected to put the farmer back on the feather bed whereon he has ridden for a hundred years—the increment in the price of farm land. All of the farm plans reduced to their lowest terms are merely attempts which have been rather vain, attempts to find some way to give the pioneer farmer what he lost when he came to the Pacific Ocean. The sad part of it is this: That increment from the price of land was a natural economic surplus. To divert a sum comparable today with the sum which once represented the economic rural surplus of an ascending spiral of prosperity under the conditions that followed the opening of new land in the nineteenth century, government in the fourth decade of the twentieth century has had to tax wealth-producing sources. The income tax has paid its toll. Various corporation taxes have been diverted to public uses and sometimes have been allotted specifically to the farmer's relief. Capital surplus taxes have been requisitioned. The last two decades, billions of dollars have been diverted directly or indirectly from their natural trend and course to relief for the farmer. But obviously the diversion of wealth to a special purpose does not produce the same results, does not answer the purpose which the natural diversion of an economic surplus produced in the pioneer economy of the nineteenth century. Indeed it is likely that wealth cannot be diverted successfully and transferred crassly from one estate of man to another, from the rich to the middle class, from the banker, the manufacturer, the investor to the farmer. It may be that we shall have to abandon the unnatural process of diversion

PECULIAR PROBLEM OF THE WEST

and direction of our economic surplus and try some other method to help the farmer. Obviously if we are to solve our national economy, it will be by producing more wealth, more goods, more substantial things to be digested naturally through social organisms of parliamentary government.

But we must remember this, and in closing I repeat it—the farmer will not be declassed. The grandson of the American pioneers will never assume a peasant's status. And possibly the solution of the farm problem is in the city—in the industrial area where idle men are waiting for an end of the farmer's depression so that the farmer may buy the things the workers make. Some day Sisyphus on his everlasting uphill job and Tantalus tortured on the rock may get together!

IV

HOW FAR HAVE WE COME—AND WHY?

BEFORE concluding this discussion about the pioneer West, it may be well to draw up a balance sheet showing gain and loss. What does it mean in the matter, first, of the physical life of the people and, in the second place, of their endowment of liberty and the pursuit of happiness?

First, how about creature comforts? How about mass luxuries? Greater physical progress the world over has been made in the last forty years since the turn of the century than was made in the hundred years before. And in this area of progress, we have moved most swiftly in the last quarter of a century. Here in the United States probably progress has come not only to the West but to all the United States, largely because we have got more power out of our fuel. We have improved and cheapened the process of making gasoline. Today we extract the heat from coal and oil much more competently than we could extract it during the last quarter of the old century. It so happens that most of our fuel has come from the area known as the West—that is to say, from the Ohio and Mississippi valleys, the Rocky Mountains, and the Pacific coast. Unbelievable volumes of coal and of oil and

HOW FAR HAVE WE COME?

also of electric energy have been developed and sold from the mines and wells of the West and from the waterfalls of the western mountains. The TVA experiment in the South, which has come into being in the last five years, is a forerunner of what is about to happen in the Rocky Mountain region. The profitable carrying capacity of one electric wire has increased in practical use both in distance and in the extended usefulness of a single wire. All these things have cheapened electricity, have in effect been getting more power out of our fuel.

It is only fair to ask how this extension of physical power from fuel has affected human life. First of all, it has been responsible for the rise of mass production, and mass production has required mass distribution. To an encouraging extent—encouraging at least to the man who believes in the evolutionary processes of democracy—mass distribution has brought myriads of new things to myriads of people.

Probably this distribution has benefited the West more than any other region. For here in the West at least we find the greatest per capita use of automobiles, of electric energy for domestic purposes; and in the West cheap fuel has been one of the major elements in throwing a network of good roads across the land. Good roads have helped the western farmer. But they have made over life in the western county-seat town even though good roads have doomed the smaller village. For western trade is centering in the western county seat. These county-seat towns of the West with a trade area covering a radius of twenty-five miles, supply the wants of twenty or thirty thousand people who come to town daily over all-weather roads. Good roads have defeated the mail-order house. It has moved a branch to the county seat. The local independent merchant in the western county seat has learned how to compete successfully with chain stores, to beat them successfully at their own game by creating new wants through alluring display of goods and by local advertising in the county-seat newspapers. These artificially created wants speed up mass distribution. The artificially created wants on the farm and in the waning villages may be economically good or bad. But they are a real part of the distribution process of the American democracy. To satisfy these newly created wants the county-seat town of the western United States has expanded immeasurably, not so much in population as in living standards. These towns are new things in the new world.

Typically the county-seat town of the West contains from 1,500 population, on the high plains east of the Rocky Mountains to 150,000 population in the rich alluvial areas of the Mississippi Valley. These western county-seat towns house their citizens more satisfactorily, give them more breathing space, provide more of the physical and spiritual blessings of life today for the average citizen than any other kind of human habitation. Certainly the western country-town dweller lives better than his farmer neighbor and much more comfortably; indeed, as an average man he lives much more luxuriously than his city neighbor, for all the city's streamlined apartments.

HOW FAR HAVE WE COME? 83

Grass and trees and flowers, accessible high schools and colleges, and a democratic spread of education produce in western country towns (which have their faults, Heaven knows) at least a more desirable physical environment than either the farmer or the average city dweller can know with an income from twelve hundred to three thousand dollars. These thriving trading points near the farm on expensive tax-built roads are the distribution agencies of American mass production. These new thriving county trade centers of the West are the social safety valves which carry forward into the twentieth century all the energy which realized the vision of the nineteenth century pioneers. The pioneer energy was balked at the Pacific. It backed up in the rising living standard of the West.

Now, what of the economic phase of this last fifty years' growth—the climax of a century and a half of pioneering? How far have we come toward the realization of the Utopia of our grandfathers who began clearing the forests and breaking the prairies after the American Revolution of the eighteenth century? "Behold," said Paul, "I show you a mystery!" And, first of all, like him I want to show you a strange and, to me, save for the spirit of our democracy, an inexplicable thing. It's the town of Emporia—population around 13,000—typifying American semiurban life, and Lyon County, Kansas, symbolizing our rural life. Twenty-seven thousand people lived in our town and county a quarter of a century ago, and the census shows almost exactly the same number of people living here now. But a survey of life at the end of this quarter of a century indicates an amazing change. It is the change in the standard of living. Our town depends almost entirely upon the surrounding county; certainly upon trade conditions in the environing state. The production of wealth in this county and state has not greatly increased in these twenty-five years. The number of acres under cultivation is about the same. The amount of brains and brawn fertilizing those acres is today what it was when Taft was President. Yet, for some reason, the vastly increased number and kinds of things we are using now in our daily lives to make them brighter and happier cost us two or three times as much as the few things we used a quarter of a century ago. In spite of this, for all our excess spending, our bank deposits have more than doubled, which shows that, with our prodigality, some way we are saving. It's crazy as a bedbug—but there it is!

ITEM 1: EQUIPMENT.—In that twenty-five years in Emporia and round about we multiplied the number of automobiles, trucks, and gasoline motor vehicles by ten. We have now more than seven thousand pleasure cars—one for every family. We had fewer than two hundred a quarter of a century ago. And the motor industry, with its filling stations, its garages, its automobile sales rooms, its stores selling accessories, has brought a new and unbelievably profitable industry into the county. Who supports it? Mostly the farmers, villagers, and local townspeople who twenty-five years ago were grumbling because they couldn't make ends meet. They are carrying on their shoulders this great new secondary automotive sales, maintenance and re-

HOW FAR HAVE WE COME?

pair industry, employing in Emporia probably upwards of a thousand people. And we are still grumbling that we can't make ends meet.

In addition to that, we have paved Lyon County with two hundred and fifty miles of all-weather roads—twenty-five miles of concrete, seventy-five of bituminous mat, and the rest of gravel or macadam—and we have paved it without issuing bonds. The state helped, but most of the help has come out of our own pockets. We have no state road debt. And in addition to these good roads, we are supporting the radio industry; but the radio is still an expensive toy—four-fifths of our people in town and country own receiving sets. We have tripled the number of telephones in use in the county. We have about as many telephones as there are houses in town and county. The telephone saturation point is reached. The radio is crowding the telephone, for eight houses in ten in Emporia, and seven in ten in the county contain radios.

With one car and one telephone for every family there is an appalling load upon the gross income of this county when one realizes that the gross production of the town and county has not increased, and taxes have risen 20 per cent! It just doesn't seem to be true, and yet the figures in the county clerk's office show that it is true. It's a fairy tale based upon reality.

Nor is that all. Emporia is the retail center of the county.

ITEM 2: GOODS.—Our stores carry larger stocks than they did in the century's first decade. Where a quarter of a century ago the turnover was two or three times a year, now the turnover is from thirty to sixty days. Instead of two or three big stores that used to get their dry goods and hardware and groceries in carload lots in great wooden boxes, now we have innumerable small shops to which ready-to-wear is shipped from New York and Chicago every week in pasteboard cartons. These hand-to-mouth stocks are sold sometimes on big special sales advertised in the *Gazette* before the cartons are burned. Here is an amazing change in this kind of merchandising business. It is nation-wide. The change, of course, requires higher transportation charges because these cartons come into town by express, by truck, by parcels post, and once in a while by air mail. A style is hardly splashed on Fifth Avenue in New York a week, before it appears on Commercial Street in Emporia and in all the Emporias of this great land. Freight has been superseded by the other transportation services in much of the merchandising; yet the car handlings of America in a quarter of a century have jumped upward as has everything else in the twenty-five-year boom.

ITEM 3: FOODS.—A quarter of a century ago, in the windows of the grocery stores were the seasonal fruits of the countryside and the vegetables grown within hauling distance of the town. In addition to that, a few citrus fruits, bananas, and at Christmas half a dozen exotic foods were hurried across the land by fast freight to feed the few rich people in the town. Now the whole year round in the grocery windows of Emporia, in thirty stores at least, are to be found always cauliflower, fresh peas, green beans, lettuce, carrots,

HOW FAR HAVE WE COME?

and great luscious citrus fruits of kinds undreamed of by our fathers. In addition to that, are avocados, melons, Japanese persimmons in season, strawberries in a long season. In the fall and winter, artichokes, brussels sprouts, mountains of spinach, Chinese cabbage and pomegranates are priced so cheaply that everyone can enjoy them. Certainly they come in quantities which makes it possible for the common man on a salary of less than fifteen hundred dollars a year to enjoy these things.

So we are better fed and better dressed than we ever were after the twentieth century's turn, and we are spending, if the number of food stores is any indication, three or four times more for food than we spent a quarter of a century ago. Moreover it's vastly better food. So unquestionably we are better clad (at least more attractively clad) and better fed and are better able to pay for our good food and decent-looking clothing than our grandfathers were, and we have more money in the bank than they had besides; even in these hard times.

ITEM 4: HOMES.—In 1912 we had a dozen or twenty big houses, houses that required two hired girls and a gardener who also was a chauffeur, for the aristocracy that owned the few motorcars in town. The local plutocrats who owned those houses are dead. The houses were changed first to fraternity and sorority houses for the college students of the town. Then, the big houses disintegrated into boarding houses. But boarding houses were displaced by hamburger joints and cafés downtown on Commercial Street. So the big houses became kitchenette apartments, and finally just naturally went to pieces. And are now for the most part old rookeries or have been torn down to save taxes.

Servant girls' wages in the day of the first Roosevelt ranged from $2 to $7 a week, and a hired man in town could be had for $20 or $25 a month and board. Now a hired girl is worth from $5 to $15 a week in Emporia, according to her talents. Home owners with lawns and gardens who have part-time gardeners and occasional chauffeurs pay $30 a month for a man about the house who doesn't work full time.

If the big house in the small town is passing, in the outskirts of every town are new "developments." Flashy, handsome little houses by the hundreds rise in the town's outskirts. These new bungalows or what not contain four to seven rooms, stuck full of electrical gadgets to help with the lighting, the cooking, the sweeping, the washing and ironing. From most of those houses the hired girl is gone. A woman comes in to clean the house Friday or Saturday. What's become of the hired girl? She's down clerking in the little ready-to-wear shops that have multiplied so fast on Commercial Street. And she's happier, she feels that she has more social status, more self-respect, and an eight-hour day. Shorter working hours and less physical grime and grind have dignified labor more than all the politicians' oratory, and with that dignity has come the chief end of it all: the growth of self-respect. For indeed the test of social progress is found in the expanding spirit of man. (Why may we not call this the democratic

HOW FAR HAVE WE COME?

spirit?) And only where man's environment affects his spirit, is a change of environment worth while. In so far as shorter hours, better wages, a wider participation in the civilization that rises from a man's toil make the man a happier, kindlier, wiser, more self-respecting man, is it worth while to struggle in the contest for social change.

Watchman, What of the Night?

I think we of these western county-seat towns have more self-respect, and we have bought it with a price. It has come with the miraculous growth of economic surplus. But where did that come from? The soil is supposed to be the source of wealth. Yet here in this county the same number of acres is being farmed by the same number of people, and they are probably taking the same gross crop income out of the soil—but not money income. Here is a brand new world. Our fathers who died in the last decade of the old century, if they could see us today, would behold here the Utopia of which they dreamed. Our grandfathers of the middle of the old century could not understand it, and our great-grandfathers would not believe it.

Yet on the other side of this picture we find too many farmers in debt. Western farm tenancy has multiplied. But even so the western farmer lives an easier life than his father knew. How does it happen? Again, "Behold, I show you a mystery," the mysterious workings of the thing we call democracy. Which brings us to the second phase of our balance sheet. Democracy means more than the ballot and the Bill of Rights. Yet the ballot and the Bill of Rights are sustaining our democracy like "the everlasting arms." It is even more than the government and the Constitution—this mystery of our democracy. But the government under our Constitution is the symbol of it all. And now, let's take some thought for a moment on the matter of how it happened, the parade—political, social, and economic —of these strange and beautiful things—the coming of a widening self-respect in American life here on our western farms and in our country towns. It has come elsewhere, of course; but I am limiting this discussion to the West.

It is necessary to look back over the fruitful years. A steady fight has been waging during the westward march of our democracy, by those who believe that a constant militant struggle to readjust our national income had to be made in view of the centrifugal tendency of capital to amalgamate. The rich indeed have grown richer. But how much does that mean? We should ask ourselves:

In this century have the rich of today grown comparatively more powerful than they were fifty years ago in the exercise of their acquisitive faculties in government, in business, and in our social life, in comparison, let us say, with the middle class? No one can deny that in twenty-five years the middle-class American has gained tremendously in comfort and in the luxuries which he enjoys. But has he along with these comforts and luxuries as much freedom of movement, as strong a voice in, say, government and business, as he had in

HOW FAR HAVE WE COME?

the days of the first Roosevelt, or of Cleveland, or of Lincoln, or of Jefferson? Again no one can doubt that the average middle-class American today is of more consequence than he was in the days of Jackson, or of Madison; of consequence in his county, his state, his nation. He is closer now than then to his mayor, his county commissioner, his governor, his Congressman and his President. Laws have been made to increase middle-class political power in the last eighty years. The trend of political change has been directed at the exaltation of political power for the average man. With more political power the average middle-class American—at least in the western democracy—has more economic substance, more social significance!

But let us take a look at American labor. Skilled organized labor normally has attained middle-class status! But what of that section of unskilled labor, insecure in employment and always on the edge of want? Has that group bettered its condition actually and comparatively?

The Rise and Fall of the "Environmentalist"

Twenty-five years ago progressive politicians like the elder La Follette and Theodore Roosevelt, whose following fairly well dominated the twenty-four western states, believed that if the environment of the underprivileged could be improved, the free exercise of their latent qualities would guarantee them a better place than they had held in the social order. We have been watching during this quarter of a century in America the struggle of the environmental theorists to reconstitute our social and economic order for the benefit of the proletariat and the fringing middle class. To that end we have been trying to use government as an agency of human welfare in education, in public service, in political weapons of democracy, chiefly to make the round plugs in our society fit into the square holes of our national economy. The environmentalists in our politics—and they included practically all the liberal and progressive leaders—were not revolutionists. They believed in the evolutionary democratic process—the political, and social and economic process. First of all, they stood for law and order. No barricades blocked the streets even in their wildest dreams.

To understand these social and political reformers of the first decade of the century it is necessary quickly to look behind them at their background. Theodore Roosevelt and Robert M. La Follette were the residuary legatees of William Jennings Bryan. They rejected Bryan's monetary theory but adopted his complaint against monopoly, particularly against the railroad monopoly and the rapidly organizing industrialists. Bryan was the child of the Populists. They were led by General James B. Weaver in 1892; and their Populist platform of that year conceived in the late eighties and early nineties, came directly out of the social vision of the Greenbackers and the Grangers. They rose and flourished in the Middle West in the seventies and eighties. This first political revolt of the farmers was almost exclusively a western uprising. It was connected closely with land—land values and farming problems—

interest rates, transportation injustices, monopolies in the buying and selling of the major commodities which affected the farmer's daily life. Back of that, before the Civil War, the slavery question overshadowed all other social reforms. So that one may say that it was fifty years ago that America's fight opened for social and economic justice—industrial justice more or less—which culminated in the Progressive, or Bull Moose, party platform of 1912. Then the sun definitely had set on the golden day of the pioneer. The West was living in an after-glow—a sentimental gloaming!

It is from there, the Bull Moose platform and the Wilson policies, both of which derived their power from the voters of the West, that we must start when reviewing the progress Americans have made in the last quarter of a century in chaining the lion of plutocratic rapacity.

It is hard to realize that a generation ago United States Senators were elected by legislatures, and that only by a subterfuge of the primary law was it possible for the people to get a direct vote upon United States Senators. It is obvious that the character of the United States Senate has changed since the adoption of the Amendment providing for direct election of United States Senators. For one thing, the Senate, since the Amendment providing for its direct election, has passed out of control of the President and the party caucus. Wilson, Coolidge, Hoover, Franklin Roosevelt have faced major rebellions of Senators in their own parties. None of these four Presidents had control over Congress toward the end of his Presidential term. Before the Amendment, the seat of political power in the United States rested in the financial districts of the cities along the Atlantic Coast. The interstate corporations—for instance, railroads, insurance companies, banking interests, the packing houses, the commodity industries, oil, coal, textiles, and the like—had in Wall Street powerful politicians who looked after their business in every state. In every state these corporations financed the political machinery of both parties. The major objective of these interstate corporations was control, first, of the state conventions of the two national parties, second, of the legislative party caucuses in the various states, that they might influence the election of United States Senators. Before the passage of the constitutional Amendment providing for the direct election of United States Senators the business leaders of the New York financial district led a strong minority of Senators also beholden directly to certain New York controlled corporations. The Wall Street alliance with American state politics furnished a lever that gave certain interested corporations great political power. They gathered grateful organized minorities in both houses of Congress, but chiefly in the Senate. The Senator who could most definitely and effectively command the services of the Wall Street boss was able with his minority of subservient Senators to control Senatorial caucuses, to say what laws should have Senatorial support, and to make definite contacts with the White House for White House patronage. The most valuable patronage of any Senator is his right to nominate to the President candidates for the federal judiciary. By controlling Senators, Wall Street was able to name

HOW FAR HAVE WE COME?

judges and make the judges as grateful as their Senatorial sponsors were grateful to the corporate "Powers that Be!"

Senator Boies Penrose of Pennsylvania was the last of the Senatorial bosses. Before Penrose it was Aldrich. Before Aldrich came Hanna. Quay preceded Hanna. And so on back to reconstruction days. Penrose, the last of the Senatorial bosses, died hamstrung and helpless when the old Senators who had been elected by legislators controlled by interstate corporations left Washington. The new Senators, uncontrolled, perhaps a cut or two intellectually below the stall-fed oxen who wore the yoke of Mammon, were restless under the old Wall Street boss. Lodge, who succeeded Penrose, had only a willow withe for scepter. Curtis, who succeeded Lodge, ruled by political combination and his own winning ways. He took few Wall Street orders. Not that he objected to them, but he knew that they could not be enforced.

Now all this is set down in detail to indicate the one significant item which is germane to this discussion; namely, the old Senate dynasty leading back to Lincoln's day was controlled by the East through Wall Street. After the direct election of United States Senators broke what might be rather amiably called the plutocratic control of the Senate, the actual control of the Senate passed from the East. In the Republican party Senatorial power went to the West; the farm bloc bossed the Senate. Later in the Democratic caucuses Senatorial power passed from the East to the South, with the West holding a balance of power.

The West in the second decade of the twentieth century with its forty-eight Senators became conscious of its power. It gave the country the income tax, prohibition, and woman suffrage. It changed the date of the inauguration of the President and the incoming of the new Congress to make responsibility to the people more effective. Prohibition was abandoned because of the growth of an urban population in the West as well as in the East. But the Amendments to the Constitution which westerners have submitted successfully since interstate corporations lost control of the United States Senate mark the influence of the West. And the rise of the farm bloc in the Senate was only another proof that the West, when it unites, can have its will and way in the American government.

In this quarter of a century we have seen other major changes come into our federal government, changes which the liberal environmentalists fathered. After Theodore Roosevelt unsuccessfully took the Progressive platform to the people in 1912, it was obvious that a third party could not exist in this country while the Electoral College remained as an institution. So the Progressive party passed. But the National Progressive Party Committee had some funds on hand and, after the election of President Wilson, moved its headquarters to Washington, where a Progressive party group began drafting bills and putting them into the Democratic hopper, bills which expressed the ideals of the Progressive party—a party which was supported largely by western liberals of both parties. Their bills became laws, and we established the Federal Trade

HOW FAR HAVE WE COME? 97

Commission, the United States Tariff Commission, the strengthened Interstate Commerce Commission, and a Communications Commission. We have hedged about, in many ways, activities which fifty years ago were the unquestioned privileges of organized wealth. The influence of the West in American politics may not have taken the wolf away from the door of the poor; but the West has certainly manicured the claws of the wolf, and he doesn't scratch so destructively as he did before the Progressive fight of 1912.*

When Wilson left the White House the conservatives walked in. But they walked into a dog fight. The western progressive bloc, voting with the Democrats when they chose and with the Republicans when the Republicans would take the progressive course, shaped most of the legislation in the third decade of the century. The West in the dusk of black reaction still was in the saddle. The West still was interested in agrarian problems. During that third decade the socialization of federal credit which began in the Wilson administration with the establishment of the Federal Reserve Act became American public policy. The western and southern farmers forced it. Federal agencies were established during that third decade to lend money (more or less government money) to farmers —western and southern farmers chiefly! And when the crash came in 1929, President Herbert Hoover took

* Most of the reforming leaders of the century's first two decades were westerners. Wilson's second election came because he carried the West. Theodore Roosevelt could not deliver his followers of 1912 to Hughes in 1916. The West was in the saddle even if it was riding a phantom horse through the afterglow of its power.

America far into the realm of socialized credit when the Reconstruction Finance Corporation was established. Benjamin Harrison and Grover Cleveland probably turned restlessly in their graves when they saw the government lending money to banks, to railroads, to insurance companies, to stabilize our economic system. Even before the election of Franklin Roosevelt, American banks were too full of government bonds. Moreover, these banks were so drastically regulated that they were virtually government agencies acting under government supervision and control and all but Federal management. The Wall Street of the ancient Senate bosses was leashed to the chariot of their former servants. Moreover, in the Hoover administration price-fixing for farm products had given agriculture a semipublic status. The farmer's wheat, corn, cotton, cattle, hogs and his land were in a way affected by public use.

Possibly this was a good thing. Possibly not. But it was opposed heartily by the centrifugal forces of organized commercial self-interest, and those forces lost their fight. Good or bad, this gradual socialization of credit and agriculture in our century's third decade indicated that the primary, the direct election of the United States Senator, and the various gadgets passing political control to the masses (certainly political ideas that came out of the West) had given the common man power to express himself in government and to make his private sentiment, public sentiment. Never before in the history of our Constitution had political power in the hands of the middle-class voter exercised

HOW FAR HAVE WE COME?

such direct influence for good or for evil upon the federal government as it has exercised in the last twenty-five years. Not since Woodrow Wilson came into the White House (scarcely for a decade before that) has any major fight in the American Congress been won definitely and certainly by the obvious forces of Mammon, except in the passage of tariff bills. In making tariffs the political horse-trader could serve his industrial masters. But even there the establishment of the Tariff Commission is at least a potential weapon to strip the winner of his victory. The West whose pioneers

> Crossed the prairies, as of old
> Their fathers crossed the sea,

has become conscious of its power. It leads the American middle class.

So much for major restrictive federal legislation. Minor laws have come out of Congress which greatly cramp the directing forces of that acquisitive collectivism which for want of a better name we call capitalism. One significant law requires certain corporations to go through the state, district and supreme courts and bars them from the lower federal district courts on all cases affecting utility rates in interstate commerce. A thousand abuses were wiped out with that statute.* Every year has seen similar cinching of the acquisitive forces in our industry and in commerce. Time and again Congress, either through legislative enactment or through its confirmation power or the power of investi-

* Sponsored by Senator Hiram Johnson of California.

gation, has seriously rebuked and crippled those who would use government as a shield for special privilege. The work of these leaders and the weight of western political pressure groups in the main has been wholesome. The power of the westerners may have been abused, but it did exist. And it was so conspicuously western that a New Hampshire Senator referred to the leaders of western liberalism as "the sons of the wild jackass."

New Times, New Men, New Issues

For statesmen in this twilight time of the western agrarianism were interested chiefly in problems coming out of the land, pioneer problems. The land coming newly under the plow, the forest falling before the ax and saw, the ore coming from the newly discovered mine, rails and wires strung over young states and piped under prairie cities, made unheard-of problems for business leaders and statesmen. And western problems, land problems, occupied the people of all the nation. In the latter half of the nineteenth century and the first quarter of the twentieth century, industrial laws in the United States lagged in legislative committees, or dragged slowly through the courts. The answer to our question—posed earlier in this chapter—about unskilled casual American labor in the days when the West controlled our politics is that it was Lazarus at the gate feeding on the crumbs from the rich man's table. Then came the army of the unemployed. With that army the problems of industry arrived. When

HOW FAR HAVE WE COME?

Lazarus rose, new leaders appeared and the rural leaders played second fiddle in the band.

Perhaps nothing more definitely marks the close of the old era, our pioneering golden age, than the change in the political leadership in Washington in the new century's fourth decade. The farm bloc which formed under Coolidge and waxed fat under Hoover, disappeared when Franklin Roosevelt brought new issues into American politics. Largely these new issues affected industry. With the first appearance in the American Congress of major industrial problems—collective bargaining, housing, hours of service, and wages, old-age pensions, job insurance—new leaders came. The leadership of the West passed. The children and great-great-grandchildren of the pioneers of the wilderness became the colts of the wild jackass. The East and South in the machine age, custodians of the great power machines, sponsors or opponents of the new day and the New Deal, are furnishing the new leadership which will try to answer our new questions.

After more than half a decade of wrestling with industrial problems, still we may ask fairly, What about the underprivileged, the man with one talent? How far is the unskilled worker's economic position determined by his intellectual equipment? How have the environmentalists succeeded in economically and spiritually benefiting the proletariat? What about the cruel social injustices which stirred the indignation of the enlightened a generation ago? Have the injustices been increased, or lessened, for those who do the rough work of our American world?

These are questions which cannot be answered by statistics. But that the underprivileged have had some share in the obvious advance of the middle class seems fairly evident. They use the roads to an extent. They occupy the motorcars. They are somewhat protected by hygienic and sanitary legislation. Their children go to school more hours per year, and to better schools, than the children of the poor enjoyed a quarter of a century ago. Ready-made clothing has given them a more attractive exterior than unskilled manual workers displayed in the days of their fathers. Except in the South among those who live on the lowest economic levels, standardized foods packaged by mass production have given the poor a little, but not much, wider diet. They have shared something (but how much?) of the benefits of our machine age which have been so bountifully lavished upon the middle class. Are not all these incidental benefits of middle-class democracy mere crumbs for Lazarus? Here is a little gain but not much, in the housing of the poor since the World War was declared, and the grosser forms of vice which ate like cancers into the poor have been checked and today are to a certain small extent removed from their environment; but this gain is only slight. As for the very poor, those who live on the indecently low economic levels, no one can say that they have shared as the middle class has shared the blessings (even the incidental blessings) nor the benefits of the American social and economic advance. Some gains, small gains, they have seen. But that is all.

HOW FAR HAVE WE COME?

Now how about the rich who are everlastingly getting richer? What is the net gain of western political leadership for three generations in the United States? The books being closed, we may ask where has the increment from the rising price of the land of the pioneers left the American people? Certainly we have more millionaires than Taft and Theodore Roosevelt knew. These exceptionally rich men live now in greater luxury than formerly. But they live less exclusively so in comparison to the near-rich and the pretentious would-be-rich and even in comparison with the substantially well-to-do, definitely middle-class burghers. Yet probably there is a wider prevalence of the conscious arrogance of unconscious class than the rich knew in the old rough-and-ready shirtsleeve days of Harriman, Frick, Schwab, Gary, and "John D. the elder." But certainly hereditary wealth takes more handicaps today than it did a quarter of a century ago. The income tax and inheritance tax cut deeply into its potential accumulations. Everywhere amalgamated wealth in the high realms of plutocratic collectivism feels the leash of democratic law even if it does not feel the ax of the revolutionary guillotine.

Have we kept up with the growing power of wealth in our democratic attempt to regulate and control industry and commerce? There again is a question. It's a guess. Evidence in plenty may be piled up to substantiate either an affirmative or a negative answer to that question. But this much is sure: There is hope, more than shadowy hope, that we are gaining on the obvious evils of the control of organized acquisitive capital. At least we recognize those evils; even the capitalists themselves, excepting a few encrusted reactionaries, realize that they are a problem. They, as well as the unemployed, are problem children.

This chapter has, in the main, arrived at the Franklin Roosevelt administration. That we have gone forward rapidly in six years with the liberal program, no one can question. That we are going further, no one can doubt. That it is an evolutionary progress is too plain to be gainsaid. Also no one may deny that in the evolutionary process we have jumped a wide gap. We are in a new era. No politicians and few business men would care to go back to the days of the Coolidge bull market, the days of the "Coolidge boom." Also the explosion of the big bull market dispelled into bankruptcy much of the wealth that our citizens had piled up in the golden age, the one hundred and fifty years of rising land values. The social ethics, the political morals, and the business philosophy of that day now have but an archaic interest. We are thinking in new social, political, and economic terms. Moreover nothing can stop the steady process of democratic evolutionary growth in our economics and in our politics, giving the average man more political power and more intelligence to use his political power for his economic welfare—nothing can slow down this movement but revolution. Our danger is not that we shall slip quietly into reaction. The menace of these last days of the fourth decade is that we may go too fast and promote reaction—make it inevitable!

HOW FAR HAVE WE COME?

What do we mean by "the steady process of democratic evolutionary growth"? That, it seems to me, symbolizes the slow assimilation of the common wealth of American people and in particular the wealth accumulated by the opening of the West. This western common wealth was distributed and digested during the country's first century and a half in something like equity by the force of public opinion. Public opinion in the democratic process enforces its decrees by many institutions, by commercial customs and traditions set by business ethics, by dicta of the churches, by the wisdom of the school and (though least significant of all) finally by laws enacted, interpreted, and applied by government agencies. Under these social institutions the social growth was achieved during which in the last century and a half the United States—conceived in liberty and dedicated to freedom—has solved problems of many kinds. Our country until the last two decades has been the hope of aspiring men all over the world. More than elsewhere these material blessings of democracy have been showered upon the middle class in the Middle West.

The political lesson of the last trek westward of the American people in the nineteenth century and the first decades of the new century is to trust evolutionary processes inherent in our democracy. They have done work that justifies the democratic faith. They are here today. These gains are the "evidence of things not seen" in the eyes of the generation that fought at Theodore Roosevelt's "Armageddon," of the earlier generation that struggled from Bull Run to Appomattox, of their fathers who died at the Alamo, and of the founders who stood beside the bridge at Concord. The visions of other days we have realized indeed as the "substance of things hoped for."

V

HOW MAY THE WEST SURVIVE?

Two thousand years ago, the young philosopher who was the founder of what by broad courtesy has been called Christian civilization, stood on a rise of ground under a great cliff at the top of a talus slope rolling toward the Sea of Galilee. There he delivered the gist and epitome of his life's creed. It was called the Sermon on the Mount. He was a skilled and powerful dialectician. That Sermon, which apparently he had prepared with all the rhetorical power of his ardent nature, was destined to be his message to mankind. That message became the philosophical groundwork of a civilization that took his name. It was not accidentally then, but with artistic premeditation that he opened this Sermon with the words "Blessed are the poor in spirit!" For the whole drift and tenor of his life and teaching urged men to that modesty, that abstention from pride and arrogance, that simplicity and nobly gentle candid courage in meeting life which is so well designated by the phrase "poor in spirit." Of course, there on the Mount, beside the Sea of Galilee, Jesus of Nazareth set forth no hard and fast rules of conduct; no minute directions for living did he proclaim. His sermon was an exhortation, the statement of an ideal, an ideal which, alas, no man and no people ever has realized, and which probably he knew never would be translated perfectly into human conduct. The nearest approach we have made as organized human beings to this idea has been made under governments where men have enjoyed the largest degree of freedom, and where reason more than force has been potent in establishing a broadening sense of justice.

In considering the survival of the West as we know that area of the United States, beyond Pittsburgh and Buffalo, on across our land through the Great Valley of the Mississippi, over the mountains to the Pacific, I like to think that men who moved into this area and have been coming there for one hundred fifty years were less hampered by tradition, less circumscribed by the lariat of formal legalities, and less bound by priest or authoritative creed, by social and economic restrictions than were the men of any other great movement of human population in recorded time. They were free in many ways—these pioneers of our American West. The rising price of land when they touched it with their plows, furnished for a century an increment which released the people in that area and kept them decently free from unnecessary penury and man-made poverty. Indeed, that increment—shall we say unearned increment?—of the land of the West was the one material blessing which brought prosperity to this whole nation, North, South, and West.

While the flood of humanity from the other American states and from northern Europe rolled westward

HOW MAY THE WEST SURVIVE? 109

over this new land, great fortunes were made in those valleys, from those mountain mines, out of those rich prairies, and upon those bleak and beautiful plains. Wise institutions were established in the West, rich commonwealths were built up, and a decent approximation of just and equitable living was established there among men. For fifty years at least, one might say broadly, but not exactly, of course, that in the civilization which our pioneers founded, were no rich nor poor. Certainly only one class, the middle class, persisted in actual dominence. The middle class lived for a generation or two upon the bounty of a virgin land, a land of veritable milk and honey. The people of that great hegira to the West did not realize whence the prosperity came which made their justice possible. They were open-handed, neighborly, kind, munificent in their beneficences, even tolerant of rapacious scoundrels; and in many cases, these westerners were regal in their institutional grant to rascals because the people, living on the rising prices of land, could well afford to be generous. But withal, the westerners did keep to the middle way of life. They did set up as their ideal of conduct a decent respect for the opinion of mankind, along with a lively sense of the blessings before them, and a rather keen appreciation of their own importance. Of course they liked to brag. In prosperity, the best of us struts a bit. But, for all of their outer brag and bluster, these western men and women were "poor in spirit." For them, this West was in truth the Kingdom of Heaven, and they loved it. They cherished their West in affection for a century and a half. But today they are baffled, bewildered, and heartsick at the inequities of this wide world—inequities which now threaten and challenge their life. I mean those deep economic and social wrongs which mock their philosophy, and which assail their democratic claims.

In that land which they love so well because it has been kind to them, because it has sustained three or four generations in the wilderness which they conquered, and because it has made what passes in their hearts at least for a Utopia, they ask themselves, "Why should all this perish?" Amid their doubts and conflicts, the children of the pioneers cry: "We thought we had established the work of our hands under God somewhat following, though blindly and falteringly, the faith that we found in the little white church, the free church standing beside the little red schoolhouse, the free schoolhouse. And on the horizon we see this great cloud of danger. What shall we do to be saved?"

Probably the answer will have to come from the little red schoolhouse. But the answer will come only if the little white church holds the fort of its faith in God and men, in the fellowship of mutual aid, faith in some kind of democratic equality of opportunity. The increment of the land that furnished the never failing reservoir of capital which kept men free, no longer flows from the rock. That rock is no longer their social and economic salvation. No longer can the prosperity of our whole country float upon the increase in the price of the virgin earth. Indeed we have fairly well demonstrated that the land itself which

HOW MAY THE WEST SURVIVE?

furnishes the food, the clothing, and the housing of our nation, the land which yielded the fabulous ore, and grew the illimitable forests, is not self-supporting. At least land is not self-supporting in the style to which we have been accustomed. If our farmers are not to be degraded into a peasantry, if they are to remain in the middle class enjoying the purely physical privileges and immunities, the educational advantages and the intellectual development of the middle class, we must fertilize the soil; we must even subsidize in various ways the business of farming. How, Heaven knows! I have no solution for the farm problem. But the problem is here. Being here, it advertises the end of reliance upon the earth and the fullness thereof to keep the economic machinery of this nation going. Working to its full, the broad acres of this land, not only of the West but of the entire country, would not produce more than enough to keep the population of the United States upon a level comparable with that of the American middle class.

It is obvious then that if the West is to survive we must find some way as a nation, particularly applicable to those vast areas that we call the West—some way to produce more goods and chattels. We must increase production if the West is to survive. Sweeping aside social vision and economic theory, getting down to the cold, hard truth about production, it may be truthfully said, I think, that the only way to increase production in this land, East, West, or South, is to get more power out of fuel. We are now getting, say about 35 per cent capacity out of our fuel. It is likely that, in the next decade, we may bring that saving of power from fuel up to 40 per cent. A visionary physicist might hope for 45 per cent.

The raising of these points in the per cent of power we can get out of fuel would add tremendously to our stock of goods, our common wealth. To increase the power of fuel, even a few per cent would add a considerable mass to our production, a mass quite comparable to the annual increase in the increment of the land of the nineteenth century. This increment was the chief source of fluid capital and incidental expanding credit which kept the West busy and established in our land a prosperity out of which for more than a hundred years we could afford a greater approximation of justice in human relations than any other nation in the world could maintain. And let me repeat, we used this increment so well under our social philosophy and with our middle-class political and business intelligence, that despite what rascals stole and what wasters scattered, we erected for one hundred and fifty years a standard of living and an ideal of justice under liberty that was the envy of mankind. Without our philosophy—let us call it frankly our religion, for our democratic faith is our religion, a phase of the Christian religion—without our philosophy, I repeat, it is fair to say that we could not have set up a schoolhouse to keep us literate and to hold us as a people fairly wise. Without that democratic philosophy which practical wisdom sustains, aggrandized power would have arrogated to itself such a per cent of the growing land increment that another civilization might have come here; a hard, cruel civilization like that which the Spaniards planted to the south of us. Under a philosophy of force, setting up tyrants on this new land of the West, a civilization might have been builded here wherein our common prosperity would have been divided among barons and profiteers and doled out to a race of slaves. That is the way many a new land has been opened.

What Is Democracy?

But the very freedom which we sought, the very justice which we yearned for, the very basic philosophy of our faith that made our morals and shaped our conduct, gave us the West that is. Heaven knows, it is far from perfection. The poor in enforced idleness today are crying for justice that comes with work. Today our democracy is challenged. Tomorrow it may be rejected. But we have a right to ask patience of those who challenge. For we are seeking the only way out. We are trying in a thousand laboratories all over the land to produce more power. When the laboratories yield their secrets, and when power is increased to produce its increment, may we not reasonably expect that the increment of increased power will produce tolerable justice under a philosophy which has worked, not perfectly, but humanly well in the last hundred and fifty years?

As we go into the employment of the many inventions that spring from the mind of man, shall the philosophy of force or the philosophy of reason be depended upon to distribute that new power? Shall the philosophy of force, diverting that power to armament, chain us as it is binding Europe to a low standard of living and to the cruel injustices thereunto appertaining? Shall we abandon our democratic faith in the new era, the era of scientific progress, this coming new pioneering era that rises like a dream come true from the embryo conceived in the little red schoolhouse? "Is the democratic process sufficient to hold science in the ways of justice?" That question contains in its answer the destiny of the thing we call the West.

Therefore, first of all, let us say what we mean by the democratic process. To me it seems that the democratic process is much more than any set of political institutions. Indeed, the democratic process writes constitutions and amends them. It does not depend on them: The democratic process operates in many ways outside of government. The democratic process is that fluidity of ideals, that dissemination of intelligence backed by purpose, that establishment of custom and folkways which seeks out and secures justice before laws come to guarantee justice. All these things constitute the democratic process in the life of a people. They are free agencies. Government is their servant, not their master. These free forces that instinctively guide a social order and establish a political government under the democratic process are slow and clumsy. Certainly they operate with vast waste. They sacrifice the tyranny of efficiency for the slower

HOW MAY THE WEST SURVIVE?

pace of the common consent of common sense, in promoting change in morals, in business, and finally in government. But the democratic process, awkward, sluggish, often sadly wasteful, and sometimes corrupt despite our ideals, does leave men free. It is slow, but it marches. It is unwieldly, but it finally wins its way.

Now what is this democratic process which has done these strange and, on the whole, beautiful things to a considerable majority of the American people? How does democracy work its changes?

It seems to me the democratic process works something like this: In every human heart are two conflicting forces, the altruistic urge and the egoistic instinct, the centripetal and the centrifugal impulses, the yearning to give and the desire to get. In every form of life these two gravities pull—even as they struggle in the movements of the stars above and in the atoms below. The final compromise in every life between these two inner stresses shapes the curve of a man's personality, marks the outlines of his character, points the inexorable pattern of his destiny. Some men on the whole are generous; others, everything considered, are mean. Here is a hero, there a villain; but in each both impulsions are hampered. No one is all good or all bad. As men socially mingle their conflicting strains, they set the moral design of the amalgamation of purpose which we know as home, or clan, or tribe, or race. In any human unit, be it home or community, be it state or region, be it nation or civilization, if on the whole altruistic social magnetisms prevail, if in any long view men are more kindly, decent, and reasonable than mean, if they are preponderantly wisely generous and noble in their prudence, then that human unit, large or small, is democratic. But if, by and large, a given human organization is greedy, if it is suspicious of everything without and credulous of everything within, if it rejects the appeal to reason and turns to force to hold its place and win its way, then that social order, under the iron law of its destiny, must turn to a tyrant for its hero and leader.

The democratic process, then, is a social order which gives freest play to that common kindly impulse of organized humanity. Man's generous instincts, alas, time often reveals, are not eternally wise. The democratic process in the end seeks to curb the egoistic instincts of men, their greeds, their revenges, their senseless fears. And these are not always ultimately evil. But the democratic process does release, so far as the wisdom of the day and time will profitably permit it, the centripetal gravities in man the individual, and in man in the mass, whether he incorporates in business, organizes in government, or crystallizes in a social order. The evolutionary processes of democracy give humanity's noble impulses a chance to function and, by trial and error, to fail or triumph.

Democracy is that type of human structure in which men of good will may have most freedom, and men who are obviously selfish must reason their way to have their will. Under the democratic order, in all the institutions which men set up in their passion for justice, the wise and kindly, decent man finds life is growing

HOW MAY THE WEST SURVIVE?

easier for him. In a democracy, business, public opinion, education, government, social customs, and religion—indeed, all man's activities—are geared to make life bearable for this decent, kindly man. In the vast interplay of conflicting and sometimes repellent forces, at the end of a day or a time or an age, life in the democratic order becomes richer, easier, fairer for the common man of good will. So justice is done. How it happens, God knows—but it happens so.

In the settlement of the West we had a fairly good working model of the play of those forces which, acting upon one another, achieved the democratic end—the school and the church. Now by the church I do not mean organized religion at all but the altruistic ethics expounded by the Sermon on the Mount. The school and the church taught by example and precept the doctrine that it pays to be kind, that it is practical to consider the so-called spiritual forces of life; meaning by the phrase "spiritual forces" the impulses rising out of the Golden Rule. On the other hand, the centrifugal forces of life that control the laws of man's self-interest, his greeds and arrogances, his fears and selfish machinations, were constantly attracted by the new sources of wealth that the western frontier afforded. Somewhat the centrifugal forces of our democratic life provided the leadership under which the new sources of wealth were created. Around all the fundamental commodities of industry were gathered in a sort of unsocial crystallization the organized grabbers and gougers. Scandal after scandal followed the swift tide of immigration in the century and a half across two thousand miles from the Alleghenies to the Pacific. The scandals of the Erie canals, the scandals of the early railroads, the Crédit mobilier, the scandal of the Standard Oil in the seventies, eighties, and nineties, the scandals of the great lumber companies that hired men to commit crime to add timber lands to the holdings of incorporated operators, the scandals of the city's real estate values complicated with public utilities, debauching our local politics, the scandals of the shoddy clothing manufacturer whose operations began in the Civil War and lasted for a generation, the scandals of railroad rebates to the interstate shippers of flour and grain, the scandals of copper in Montana and Arizona—all these scandals made it plain that the centrifugal forces were trying to tighten the hold of self-interest upon the common wealth of the American people. It was human nature for leaders of an enterprise to believe that they were its sole owners and to act accordingly. The two forces fought through the century. But in the end the meek inherited the earth. In the end an approximately just social control bound the aggrandizers into some fair semblance of a just and equitable relation to organized society. That struggle was the democratic process. It was at work not only in city councils, in legislatures, in the Congress, not in politics alone, nor chiefly. That struggle between the over-acquisitive and the meek was in the hearts of the American people who were settling the West, building up a democratic civilization. Man being what he is—in the main naturally a bit lazy, in-

HOW MAY THE WEST SURVIVE?

stinctively inclined to improvidence, by birthright glad to let well enough alone—what else can man do but reward the exceptional few: those who goad him to work, those who shame him to save, those who drag him out into today's danger for tomorrow's prosperity.

The best that mortal and easy-going man can do is to work out some kind of biological, social, or political unit by which the leader gets the lion's share for his necessary services; then, when the lion grows slothful in his pride, take it away from him. This is the secret of democracy: the democratic man knows that, when the lion's work is done and the lion's share is taken and the lion gets old and fat, he is just another human, and he cannot guard his lair. So justice raids his cave and evens things up, and the world moves on. The lion who in another era was a soldier, then the king, then the priest, and now the plutocrat, has waxed fat, grown greedy and lost his power. This is the way of democracy. Has man wandering in this worldly wilderness ever devised a better system than ours for making the desert blossom as the rose? I am inclined to think that this age-long yearning for justice, this deep desire of humanity to promote justice through liberty, giving the strong man his freedom and his reward while he works and then, when we learn his secret, profiting by his achievements and sharing his gains—as I say, I am inclined to believed that this old, old order ever expanding, ever redistributing the rewards of common work within the human herd, in short, this democratic civilization, is a special organism in the life of man.

How Doth the Little Busy Bee?

To explain a little more lucidly than I have done heretofore about the function of democracy in the settlement and growth of our American West, here is what I mean by this democratic order as "a special organism." Biologists and biochemists hold that an organism has three qualities, three capacities: the power to feed itself; the power to reproduce itself; the power to protect itself. Translated into slightly emotional terms, this means that an organism has its hungers, its loves, its defenses. Unquestionably, in the higher forms of life the tree, perhaps the forest itself, is an organism. The individual vertebrate mammal is an organism, and so is the herd. The bird is an animal organism, and so is the flock. The bee is an organism, and so is the hive. The forest, the herd, the flock, the hive, all have their own laws, their own hungers, their own ways of reproduction, their own defenses. The human body is an organism. Why should we not say that the clan, the tribe, the nation are human organisms. May we not reasonably assume that one of the higher organisms of human association is this new thing that has been growing in the world for three thousand years, this thing we call democracy? It has its hunger, which is the aspiration for justice. Democracy has its capacity for reproduction, which is the extension of justice by reason. It has its power of defense, in the reasoned potency of its ideals. Obviously democracy, like the forest, the herd, the flock, and the hive is trying to make its own pattern, trying to establish its own conceptions of justice.

HOW MAY THE WEST SURVIVE? 121

Set deep in human hearts, as the instinct of the bees makes the curious geometrical pattern of the honeycomb and the inner forms of the life of the hive, so democracy instinctively is working out some pattern of human conduct in human association. It is clumsy. It is slow. It is mysterious in its purpose and direction, this democratic instinct. Essentially and at the bottom, it is an altruistic impulse—the desire for equality based upon a sense of fraternity. This impulse for justice cannot be set up by force entirely. It requires faith, faith in man, faith in the decency of the average man, faith in man's intelligent self-interest, faith in his final compliance with the social pattern of democracy. How shall we establish this social pattern of democracy? It is by no means worked out and determined but is in its evolutionary stage—perhaps only a secondary stage. Yet if we can hold democracy in its place on the globe, we shall in another day, in another generation, perhaps in another century, approach the social pattern intuitively set deep in the heart of man, in his aspiration for social and industrial justice! Where the lion shall lie down with the lamb!

Exactly what I mean by the social pattern of democracy is this: Twenty-four states west of the Alleghenies, outside of the South, were organized in the century and a half following the adoption of our American Constitution. Obviously the men who went into those states were free men. They had a wide latitude of freedom under which they might have established several kinds of commonwealths. If, on the whole, the egoistic forces struggling for supremacy with the altruistic urge in man had won here or there or elsewhere, we might have had deviations in the kind of life which one commonwealth established. Here, say, in the wide expanse of Montana might easily have been set up the hacienda system which prevailed southeast of the Rio Grande. There in Utah where a strange variant of the altruistic dogma would have established polygamy and did set up a form of theocratic socialism, we might have had imbedded in the state constitution some strange modification of the pattern of liberty which was set in the other states. In Kansas, born in the fanatic struggle against human slavery, the constitution and the way of life of the people might have been twisted or warped into the establishment of intolerance. But no, in governmental pattern the states are all alike, as nearly alike as the cells in the beehive. Yet each western state has its own geographical peculiarities, its own social distinctions, its own economic idiosyncrasies. But they are all blended into a common life, the continental organism that we call the American democracy. It is a scientifically exact and typical biological organism of its own kind.

One more limitation must be set down in the definition of the democratic ideal: At base government is force. Even in a competently working democracy, government still is force. Government is sheer force in the hands of the owners (or their political agents) of such goods, chattels, and vested interests as at any given time shall be agreed upon as private property. Government is force to protect that property legally from invasion. But it is the essence of democratic

HOW MAY THE WEST SURVIVE?

freedom first to hold open a wide zone in which property rights are admittedly dubious and then to permit full and fair discussion of the justice of those dubious rights. In an evolutionary social order—such as Americans maintained in the frontier days of the West—the twilight zone of property rights is always narrowing. The debate between the haves and the have-nots in the United States, and particularly in the western United States with its amazing Golconda, has been untrammeled for a century and a half. That stabilizing force which is government has protected the haves in much that they hold. On the other hand the free play of altruistic challenge within the debatable area of private property rights, has done three important things: First, it has set up a substantial satisfied growing middle class. Second, freedom to discuss and under reason to narrow the rights of private property has given even the most acutely underprivileged group—Marx's proletariat—a sense that their case is not hopeless. In the frontiersman's West the poor man's case was really hopeful. This sense that even for the worst of us things are changing for the better, has kept down barricades and has checked radical and revolutionary movements. And third, the freedom of discussion in the challenge of property rights and the constant narrowing of property rights as wealth has been increasing from the farms and the mines and the forest of the fecund West, has kept our plutocracy—with its lion's share—pretty well in its place. Class arrogance in our democracy is bad form on both sides of the middle class. Passing through the middle class, the competent proletarian going up or the incompetent plutocrat coming down, is purged of his caste feeling. The individual freedoms sustained by the constitutional Bill of Rights make in our democracy a cushion of self-respect. This self-respect prevents chain-galls that might sear the body politic if the citizen realized too often and too acutely that government is force, force that holds the have-nots from the treasure of the haves. For when the dispossessed are free to talk, and do talk the privileged out of some of their property every decade or so, the liberties of democracy become the balance wheels of the machinery that generates law and order. The rampant freedom of the wild and woolly West of our pioneer ancestors, raw and vulgar as it often was, none the less acted as the safety valve of American civilization. It was our "peculiar treasure"! Under the cooling shades of that western freedom the people of the United States met and solved, with something like justice, the problems that might have overwhelmed us; the problems that arose from the undigested wealth amassed by our nineteenth century pioneers.

Our next question arising out of the problem of the settlement of the West and the survival of the West is more serious than the other: Is this democratic process strong enough, and are its purposes clear enough, its ideals reasonable enough, to keep the larger freedom that is needed for the triumph of democracy? I mean the freedom of science, the essential freedom of enterprise and invention, the initial freedom of the exceptional man who in our democratic organism must take leadership, must have responsibility, must be un-

HOW MAY THE WEST SURVIVE? 125

hampered so long as he is honest in the use of his ten talents, his magic gifts, his extraordinary powers. The trouble with tyranny, with despotism, with the totalitarian order is that, whether the dictatorship be of the proletariat, or of the plutocracy, or of the military arm of the state, any tyranny makes the man of ten talents the slave of the dumb tyrant who holds his job by reason of his arrogance, his ruthlessness, and his cunning. The totalitarian state is doomed not because it enslaves the men of one talent and regiments the men of five. The totalitarian state is doomed because it hampers, checks, tries to guide and control the man who under the free democratic process, by reason of his talents and powers, may assume leadership and give direction to the life about him. I mean the inventor, the enterpriser, and the statesman, the financier—the lion among men—the genius who comes every decade in every generation to function in the hive and hold the democracy to its ideals as a human organism. I would keep him honest, of course. He should give back to society full social return for the privileges he enjoys. But after that, the leader as he works should be free. He is the problem child of this generation where modern democracy is slowly forming its organic character, ready to take its place in the development of humanity.

Our Modern Problem

What is our immediate American democratic problem down at the roots of it? Even in the farming West it is essentially an industrial problem. If we establish industry upon an equitable basis, we shall have done the best we can do for the farmer. For an equitable basis in industry presumes that labor shall no longer be sold in an open market as a commodity. If we are to distribute the benefits and blessings of the growth of fuel power which will increase our production, we must give to labor a new status, an enlarged status as a consumer of goods and chattels. Lincoln, with a scratch of the pen, started the political institutions which unshackled American labor. When labor was emancipated, under Lincoln's impulse, when a man could sell his labor in an open commodity market, our fathers said seventy-five years ago, "At last man is free!" But man is not free today, offering his labor in a commodity market. Man cannot bargain alone on anything like equality, justice, or fraternity, with a buyer of labor who represents a great corporate industry. The collective bargaining power of labor must be firmly established. Only that firm establishment of the collective bargaining power of labor will give labor self-respect. But with that self-respect must come an increased share in the products of labor. Then the self-respecting workingman may consume up to his capacity to earn the things that shall come pouring out of the mills and factories as well as the products of the American farm in the new day when we shall enlarge the productive capacity of man by squeezing more power out of fuel.

What will stop that increase in the consuming power of the manual worker? It seems to me that the chief impediment just now to industrial progress is the arrogance of certain blind owners of the tools of industry. I believe in capitalism. I do not believe in a proletarian ownership of the tools of production, nor anything like it. It has not worked under the tyrannies of Europe, neither in Russia, nor in Central Europe. Labor really asks little. When a man decides to be a worker, consciously or unconsciously he makes the decision not to go after money and the power of money as his life's first aim and instead elects to live by the work of his hands. Right then and there the average American worker indicates definitely that he will be happy with a middle-class status. By a middle-class status, I mean exactly this: A decent house equipped with modern comforts and a few luxuries, good food, respectable clothes, an education for his children which shall include high school and, if the son or daughter desires it, a college education. In addition to these decencies workingmen require and are beginning to demand security against sickness, old age, and unemployment. These things, these rather simple middle-class blessings, will satisfy labor. And if the workingman has these elements of self-respect, they will make labor a sufficient consumer to take up the slack in the consumption of goods that will come out of the new powers that men shall wrest from the forces of nature.

What holds back the realization of that ideal? It is employers' fear and greed: a fear that is a phantom; a greed that is a curse. Let me develop this answer: In settling the West we absorbed democratically the great increment of the land values. We have established in our

West, during one hundred and fifty years of freedom, a civilization far from perfect, but a workable civilization in which men have risen and fallen in some relation in their capacities, and in some measure of justice. Moreover we can continue this measure of justice in the new pioneering age of the machine, if only the boss, the man who owns the tools of industry, will have faith in his country, faith in his fellow man. We ask only that the capitalist—the man who owns the tools of industry—shall have the faith that turned the wilderness of the West into a fairly civilized land. In that faith he may go on to the next evolutionary stage of democratic progress. But he must have faith, this inventor, this enterpriser, this owner of the tools of production. He must have faith that democracy as a permanent human organism can survive only if a considerable majority of any democratic unit—from the family to the nation—share the blessings of democracy. This does not mean share and share alike.

The equality of democracy is equality of opportunity which in modern terms should include the right to be as well born physically as the average child. It should include the right to be educated well enough to put an intelligent vote into the ballot box. Democratic opportunity should give to every citizen a right to work, preferably in private industry, but if not that then the right of self-respect in earning his bread. Democratic equality cannot, and certainly should not, try to level men down, nor to establish a social, political, or economic order that will ignore in its material rewards the deep differences in the qualities of men.

HOW MAY THE WEST SURVIVE?

But equality of opportunity does assume to every citizen a decent environment, working conditions as safe and as wholesome as science can make them, a government that assures the citizen personal safety, equality before the law, civil liberty, the blessings of public sanitation and hygiene, and some security against the inevitable hardships of old age. These things the democracy of the western pioneers did fairly well—as well as a civilization could do that was afoot and moving.

But now a settled civilization has a call to do these things well. The point about the tool owner's faith in this enlarging democratic process is that he must purge himself of delusions about an ironbound wage fund. He must cut loose from the Stone Age economic theory that the metes and bounds of certain funds, wages, interest, profits, and the like can be gauged in advance by known laws and prophetic rules. Economic rules are inviolable, but the conditions under which economic laws work vary from year to year. Valid restrictions in one day and time hold nothing that is inexorable for another. Pragmatic experience, and that alone, will point out the boundaries of the possible and the impossible in all institutions, all aspirations and ways of life, all progress in government, in business, in human associations. That, men of five and ten talents must realize. In the faith of that realization they must walk like Shadrach, Meshach, and Abednego into the fiery furnace of the tomorrow. Democracy as a going concern has survived change, progressive economic change.

Democracy will survive if it inspires man's spirit, if

change guarantees to all men, those who toil and those who direct toil, the liberties necessary to self-respect. Faith in that truth is not wanting in those who have little to lose. But those who risk much will gain more if they move forward in democratic faith into the next stage of our national development. Even as their fathers before them—the pioneers in our wilderness—came into broader usefulness and into more competent power, in the wider distribution of democratic blessings than they had under the older order in the elder days. It should be so in the expanding democracy that will come with the enlargement of machine power that may come tomorrow. I seriously fear, as I have already indicated, that the problem child of our democratic civilization today is not the labor racketeer (who is only a nuisance with all his nagging demands for the tool workers) but rather the man in the front office, the man at the flat-topped desk, the capitalist, the owner, whether he be a soulless corporate entity or a finite man mildly mad with a delusion of the danger to his property rights.

One would think, to hear the clamor from the owners of the tools of industry and their banker backers, that property rights had never changed in this country. One might imagine, listening to the hubbub of the property owners, that every property right that ever existed in the United States was set in the cement of the American Constitution. The truth is that nothing is more unstable than property rights under our American government. Property rights affecting many kinds

HOW MAY THE WEST SURVIVE? 131

of property have shifted many times since the beginning of the migration across the Alleghenies to the West. One hundred fifty years ago, the man with a dollar had a legal and moral right to buy votes with his dollar in the United States. When his right was questioned, the property owner lifted a voice of angry protest at the threat of anarchy. A little later, the property right of the American investor who owned apprenticed or indentured labor vanished, amid the owner's predictions of approaching doom for orderly civilization. A few decades after indentured labor passed, the property right of men in human beings was wiped out after the Civil War. Wisdom on both sides, warned of that conflict, might have made the war unnecessary and still would have abolished that property right in slaves; but pride on one side and malice on the other built up a dam of hate and avarice which it took a revolution to dislodge. Forty years ago the property owner who had invested his dollar in railroad stocks and bonds, cried "Socialism!" when his property right to make railroad rates as he pleased was menaced by government. He had a secure property right in 1880 to give rebates, to set up privileges for cities, for states, for regions by setting up preferred railroad rates according to his will. That property right passed. A few years later, the railroad investor lost another valuable right—the right to issue passes, passes which influenced politicians who controlled the machinery of our city, state, and national governments. The pass privilege as a property right disappeared thirty years ago. Then, when those rights passed, the threat to the flag which the property owner imagined when his property right passed, never was fulfilled.

A generation ago, when Theodore Roosevelt came to the White House, men had a property right to sell any kind of food which they could fool the buyer into paying for in the market. With the adoption of the Pure Food and Drug Act of 1906, which was denounced as pure socialism, that property right to swindle food buyers passed, and the old red, white, and blue flag still waved over the land of the comparatively free. The property right of the investor in swindling schemes or questionable merchandising methods was greatly restricted when the government at Washington set up the Federal Trade Commission. The foundations of the Republic, which were supposed to crumble when the act was passed, are still intact. When the income taxes took away from the well-to-do man the right to spend his own dollar in his own way, one would have thought to hear the uproar that preceded the adoption of the Constitutional Amendment, that the hordes of destroying Vandals were at our gates. But after that restriction of property rights, God reigned and the government at Washington still lived. When the parcels post was established, the property rights of dollars invested in express companies and railroads again were limited. But nothing happened. Property rights under our Constitution keep shifting and changing. Men smart enough to acquire property and hold it keep getting and holding more property, while those who have no property sense benefit a little from the

HOW MAY THE WEST SURVIVE? 133

changing status of property. The forces of egoism as opposed to the forces of altruism are in constant conflict in our political, social, and economic life. It is necessary to restrain the egoistic forces. For power fosters greed. If the egoistic forces of democracy are absolutely unfettered, greater evils will come than those that follow the restriction of the property rights of those to whom an expanding machine age has given power. But about all that happens in a democracy concerning shift of property rights is this: Men who like property well enough to pay for it get it; men who like something else better than property generally get that also. So expanding democracy marches on. The reverse sides of our great seal of state should show these heraldic pictures: on one shield—old Daniel Boone, the wilderness pioneer, in coonskin cap, couchant, with rifle on knee, peering prophetically westward, where he sees on the other shield the test tube rising rampant, the microscope, the armature, grouped. Between the two shields this motto should shine:

O Boss, Owner, Enterpriser, O Capitalist: Live Forever! For Democracy Always Has Worked Fairly for You. It Always Will. Keep Your Shirt On!

We are reaching another stage of readjustment of the rights of property like that which occurred in the eighties, when railroad owners lost some of their unsocial property rights, and later under the first Roosevelt and in the Wilson administration, when they lost certain predatory rights. Every generation must make its own adjustments, "lest one good custom should corrupt the world." Our generation seeks to curtail the property rights of the machine owner in his dealings with labor, with the investing public and with the consumer of machine-made goods. We make that property restriction in laws controlling somewhat the wages and hours of labor, laws guaranteeing to labor the unhampered right of collective bargaining. Today we are also curbing the egoistic rights of property in regulating the corporate organization of property owners who hold public utilities stocks and bonds. We are limiting property rights by controlling stock exchanges and grain markets. We are seeking to restrict or at least control monopoly. This does not menace the stability of the American government. Readjusting property rights to define new limits of social, legal, and business honesty does not threaten the continuance of American institutions, nor imply a change in the course and aim of American life any more than those other restrictions impeded our progress, thirty, fifty, seventy-five, or a hundred years ago. Yet these ancient reforms were adopted despite the pious and patriotic shrieks of property owners.

The Problem Child of Democracy

Today as we plunge into the new frontier which is marked by the smoke of the laboratory, the frontier which is to increase our power of production by increasing the percentage of use we can get out of fuel, we must necessarily change property rights as they were changed in other days and in other times. If these rights remain static, they establish injustice.

HOW MAY THE WEST SURVIVE?

In a day of inevitable and universal change, only a static condition in any part of society menaces the perpetuity of democratic society and overthrows balance which comes with change. It is hard to make the owners of industrial machines, of seats in the stock exchange, of stocks in utilities, and of bonds see these things. Their vanity in their great power blinds them. Alas, it is power, and the vanity of power seeking to dam the flow of democratic currents which gives revolutions their impetus, as hate breeds hate and arrogance fosters envy. Thus class wars have arisen through the long centuries of human history. It should be the hope of patriotic Americans that we can cross our new frontiers today using the same democratic common sense, with the increment of new wealth which we used crossing the old frontiers into the old wilderness. If only we can command those forces of struggle between conflicting instincts which stabilized and democratized the huge economic surplus that rose out of the pioneering days of our fathers, we may today go forward into the new changes that are about to greet us. We may meet tomorrow without fear. But our problem child, the man in the front office, the man who controls for the hour but does not own our great corporation, must become definitely conscious that in saving his face, his pride is begetting timidity. His class timidity will beget class greed which in turn will blind him and his kind to the claims of justice and to the ideals of a free fight for adjustment under fraternity upon which our democratic government was founded, in which our American way of life is set.

It takes all kinds of men to make a world, men with many qualities. In our world today there is a place for all these men, and for even nonacquisitive men, who should be equitably but of course not equally rewarded. No one wants, no one but a fool would try, to establish a social and industrial and economic system upon the basis of equality of social rewards. "In my Father's house are many mansions!"—luxurious apartments, comfortable cottages! In our democracy, why should the man of ten talents, because he is only one in ten, fear the man of one talent even if he is ten to one? Justice may be established between the one man and the many by the use of reason more surely than justice may be decreed by force. People in the long run have sense.

Time and again, in the settlement of the West, has it been made clear that a social order may be erected and maintained under the capitalistic profit system—an order founded upon justice, upheld by reason and not too crassly by force, an order deeply underpinned and founded instinctively upon what has been called "sweet reasonableness and the will of God." It will not work perfectly, of course. There will be flaws, blots, and blemishes. But as our old West worked fairly well despite the rascal, in the face of the pillage of the plunderer, in the distribution of the unbelievable billions of dollars of increment from the land, so the new West will work if it is underpinned with the democratic faith in what passes for a Christian civilization. We can, if we will, here and now under democracy create an equitable order for the distribution of

HOW MAY THE WEST SURVIVE?

the stupendous increase in human wealth that is rising from the enlargement of mechanical power with its increase of production.

Concluding, let me reiterate that what man did with that fabulous increase in wealth that came with the settlement of the West, man can do now as he plunges into the new era. But he must carry in his heart the two things that made the wilderness blossom as the rose: first, a neighborly faith in the decency of man; second, a never faltering vision of a better world. That vision the pioneers had—even the worst of them. That vision always must shine in the depths of man's heart if he moves on to those broadening liberties that follow expanding duties. It is the essence of democracy. The more liberties we enjoy, the more duties we assume. That vision, dearly beloved, of justice in human relations, is what was meant when it was written: "The kingdom of God is within you." Raw force never will set up that kingdom! Our way of life here on this continent today with all its obvious inequities, with its many cruel shortcomings, still is the Utopia that glowed in the heart of the pioneers. We have conquered much along our westward march during the century and a half—much of oppression, something of greed, a lot of foolish or wicked inequalities. But these conquests were on the battlefield within man's expanding spirit. It was the democratic process—conflicting forces in the human heart reaching a final equilibrium in approximate justice.

The man of ten talents is beginning to show an understanding heart. But our leadership must have the vision that has sustained even the poor, the underprivileged. Our men of exceptional qualities must hold the eternal hope of a just world which has inspired all human progress. America is ready for the next forward step, when the increment that comes from mechanical power shall replace the surplus of wealth that rose from the settlement of the West. But progress today is only possible if into the heart of our man of ten talents, into the heart of the boss, sitting before the single rose on his clean glass-top desk can come that first amazing word of the young preacher on the Mount who opened his discourse with that passionate exhortation to humanity across the centuries, "Blessed are the poor in spirit, for theirs is the kingdom of heaven!"

VI

THE NET OF IT

Despite the agony, the terror and the disillusion that have come with the world wide challenge to the democratic ideal in the second quarter of the twentieth century, probably the challenge had to come. For only in answer to challenge after the hard pragmatic test of actual living could we know certainly that the democratic organism has its reliance not in laws, not governments, nor even the customs of a civilization, but rather in dependable human qualities. Democracy is such a new thing in mankind's journey over this earth! As a vision even now hardly developed into a theory, the democratic ideal has been inspiring sages and statesmen probably only two or three thousand years. The rule of force governed men when they first came out of the forest and began to live on their herds and later on their crops. But until man's toil produced more than his daily need he could ill afford the luxury of that neighborly generosity which is the basis of every reasonable society. Indeed, the rule of reason replacing force has guided governments controlling any considerable part of humanity for less than a third of a thousand years. It was the new era when men were developing fire, the wheel, the lever, to wide usage and establishing private and corporate partnerships to spread universal commerce. They made in these recent times more things than they needed for the day, the season or the year. As men in great masses turned into Easy Street, they began to realize that they could afford neighborly relations. Men began to consider, reason things out, to share with the weak, to curb the unsocial strong, and not live the greedy lives to which the millions of the poor have been doomed for thousands of years. In that brief flicker of time, the machine age, democracy has spread a thicker veneer of reason over a small part, at least, of the life of the people—thicker than the vast majority of human beings had known in other centuries.

Even now some of the conduct of all of humanity is moved by force. In the great democracies, force is used to hold millions in check whose unintelligent instincts would run riot if force were removed from government and law. Yet governments extending over probably half a billion people in the British Dominions, in the United States, in France, Belgium, the Netherlands, and the Scandinavian countries and to some extent in Latin-America, are founded on an ideal of reasoned justice to the common man, an ideal of reasonable relations in the routine of daily life. Kindness as a way of self-respecting neighborly association is protected by laws and business customs in these democratic lands. Whether protection comes with the ballot box, the writ of habeas corpus and the Bill of Rights, or not, is hardly of first importance. Though those guarantees of personal liberties are precious. But democ-

THE NET OF IT

racy simmers down to this essence: It is the freedom of the common man to be neighborly in any relation of life, and the freedom of the exceptional man to be useful in every honest endeavor that calls him. In democracy all men, strong or weak, wise or dumb, have the precious right to be neighborly to rich or poor, to Jew or Gentile, black or white, to Catholic, to Protestant or atheist, to fellow patriot or foreigner.

The question which is contained in the modern challenge of democracy is this: Do modern men finally in their relations with their fellows intuitively prefer to be free, to be kind and useful in their own way, after their own light and leading, following their own consciences, guided by their own judgments, or do they prefer to have their conduct and their neighborly duties exactly and minutely channeled by whatever ruler the day and the times may produce; let us say— by the detailed regulations of a socialistic state, by the carefully, scientifically worked out proclamation of a dictator, or by the rigors of military orders.

Man is an easy-going animal. Most men in the mass are sluggish spiritually, lazy physically. Often a leader rises whose exceptional energy is guided by exceptional intelligence. He takes charge of his docile neighbors. Their noblest purpose—and his—move them with his surplus energy. Probably the only differences between new democracy and old tyranny is that modern political leadership of mankind in western civilization on the whole has tried to reason men into walking in the ways of peace and something approaching justice. It has been a comfortable journey and "we who are still on our pilgrimage" have been widening our sympathies, growing benevolent habits of thought and action. Here and there we have formulated our habits into rules of conduct, into laws and constitutions which are erected to preserve the greatest possible justice among men with the least possible show of force. Our leaders particularly in these last three centuries have become heroes only as they have incarnated the rising spirit of altruism. The rise of neighborly benevolence has been one dominant social tendency of this modern machine age—the democratic era.

Now a new kind of leader is rising in the world. New heroes are challenging this easy, clumsy, ineffective tolerance which is the essence of democracy. These new shining heroes of the totalitarian states who make efficiency their god and scorn democratic waste are having their say. They are speaking from the mouths of cannon. Their winged words drop as bombs upon fear-stricken cities. These new leaders are on the march. Their doctrine of dictatorial force is overrunning the boundaries of weaker states.

Democracy is mobilizing to defend itself on a score of fronts and with many weapons. As these lines are written, even the terms of democratic survival have been stated rather vaguely. But the dictator's war cry is calling like Goliath's to David's supporters. Democracy will define its terms more clearly as the year grows older and the decade ends. The answer finally will not depend upon guns. It will depend upon the resilience of the human spirit. Whatever terrain the gods of battle may win or lose, democracy will rise or fall only if the common man, for all his laziness, in spite of his mass shiftlessness, his ne'er-do-well ways, definitely decides in his heart that the democratic way of life is a good way. Then the expansion of the human spirit manifesting itself in God only knows what strange ways shall burst the chains of tyrants and free mankind. Nothing can resist the resilience of the human spirit, if the expanding spirit of man is a reality and not an illusion. If in the seed of our first crudest civilization the pattern of democracy really was implanted in our hearts, then nothing, not embattlements and fortifications, not airbirds dropping their poison eggs, not the will of tyrants nor their chains will hold men from faith in the love of their individual liberties and their sense of their neighborly duties. In short if democracy is a human organism nothing can check nor divert the slow mighty forces from within that are inherent in man's high destiny.

Let strong men be mean. Let weaklings be lazy and envious. Let the mediocre man be complacently befuddled. So it has been always. Put them to work side by side—the grasping, the do-less, the bewildered. A hidden grace in each of them—perhaps tolerance or a shamefaced nobility or maybe an innate sense of fairness—amalgamates their baser qualities. A patent of social conduct emerges, strange and full of friendly purpose. They who seem to be pulling and hauling, jostling and clamoring have done a day's work that is somehow good. But they only are as competent and wise as they are free. So the wisdom of kindness—let's call it the love of man—comes to bless their labor.

We must take this love on faith today. But it is an ancient faith. Moses eagerly followed it as a rule of conduct to the burning bush. Plato defended it as an ideal against Dionysus. Jesus expounded this faith and died for it. It is the light of the world.